Dealing with Racism

Dealing with Racism

A coloured man's perspective on the personal and collective journey to a truly free South Africa

NATHANAEL SILJEUR

I dedicate this book to my children Jesse, Jordan and Joshua.

To God be the Glory.

TABLE OF CONTENTS

INTRODUCTION

Defeating racism, tribalism, intolerance and all forms of discrimination will liberate us all, victim and perpetrators alike.

—Ban Ki-moon:
Former United Nations Secretary-General

Racism is a global phenomenon. First-world countries and developing countries are struggling with how to implement anti-racism measures and how best to achieve non-racialism and social cohesion. This book focuses on the areas of our daily lives and how we could assist and should assist in the development of a racially integrated society where the dignity of each person, especially the most vulnerable – our children, are protected.

At this point in South Africa, it seems mistrust amongst racial groups is high. The land debate is making some people anxious and angry. The land debate has strengthened the polarisation of different ethnic groups. However, it is not only in South Africa that race relations are under pressure. In America, the President has uttered racist comments and law enforcement organisation racist practices have led to the killing of many young black men. In Britain, they are struggling with structural racism. However, in Canada, there seems to be light at the end of the tunnel. In the province of Ontario, they have developed a systemic and strategic three-year plan to combat racism.

This book provides a brief understanding of the coloured identity in South Africa while also offering a discussion on racism and the pragmatic steps we can take in combatting it. The book will hopefully provide an opportunity for readers to obtain new perspectives on these subjects and perhaps even to change their own beliefs around what can be done as parents and individuals to combat racism and promote non-racialism.

Further advice and recommendation are supplied using questions we should be asking and books or publications we should be reading to educate ourselves further.

This book reflects my viewpoint regarding racism through the lived experiences as a coloured person during the apartheid era and in the democratic period in South Africa. Further, I attempt to provide recommendations regarding how we could combat racism and not poison the future of our children. This book is not written for academics but hopefully will make a small contribution towards the eradication of racism while also providing a better understanding of the story of the coloured people.

The book challenges our beliefs regarding human dignity and equality and asks essential questions about our personal beliefs and our own commitment to ensuring human dignity and equality in South Africa and the eradication of racism. The second, more fundamental, question requires us to ask ourselves what we can personally do to help achieve these objectives in South Africa.

Shortly before writing this book a media story appeared that epitomised the racial conflicts seething under the surface of our society. In this story, a South African citizen named Adam was holidaying on a Greek island and decided to make a video showing us the beauty of the island's beach. What made the beach particularly beautiful for Adam was that there were no "kaffirs".[1] The word "kaffir" is highly offensive in South Africa and is a racial slur that denigrates the dignity of African people. The video caused a media storm and had a significant negative impact on Adam's family's businesses and his relationship with his siblings, parents, children and nieces and nephews. Immediately, his family started receiving death threats. Family members felt hurt and ashamed and took the commendable step of publicly condemning the behaviour and the words expressed by their son and brother. The perpetrator's written apology was also the first step in the right direction.

However, democratic South Africa has continuously struggled with racism. A highly critical report produced by the South African

Human Rights Commission (SAHRC) in 1999 emphasised that much needed to be done to root out racism.[2] It stated that four years into democracy, widespread reports of racism persisted.[3] In the same year, a separate SAHRC investigation found evidence of racism in the media and at universities.[4]

The roots of racism are deep. Between 28 August and 5 September 2001 South Africa hosted the World Conference against Racism, Racial discrimination, Xenophobia, and Related Intolerance in Durban. The gathering had many excellent outcomes, but racism persists, and in the last two years we have heard of more and more incidents.

Why?

I want to explore this and suggest pragmatic steps that we, as ordinary South Africans, should be introducing to eliminate racism from our society. And I want to do this from the particular perspective of being a coloured man. The very term "coloured" is itself conflicted and will need to be explored with care.

Even my siblings and I have different viewpoints on the coloured identity. One Saturday my siblings and I were braaing with our families and the discussion turned to what it meant to be coloured and how we should address racism in South Africa.

Sebastian, my younger brother, is married to Antonia, a Dutch national, and they have a son. One of my questions was, does their son identify as coloured? Sebastian explained that their son must determine that for himself and that he releases his son from the history of apartheid and the "baggage" of the coloured identity. I found myself inwardly disagreeing, but I made the effort to listen and understand his viewpoint.

My eldest brother, Emmanuel, identifies strongly with being African and with an African consciousness. However, I identify strongly with being proudly coloured.

Emmanuel wants the racial classifications used on our official forms to be African African, African Coloured, African Indian, and African White. We try to explain the current legislation, but he passionately advocates that each citizen identity should be rooted in being African.

Antonia says she ticks the "Other" box because she does not consider herself as white but as European.

So, within my coloured family, and indeed the coloured population, you will find a lack of consensus about the term coloured and may encounter some real hostility to this label. What my brother said is so true. Writing this book will cause many emotions and especially with regards to the terms "coloured", "coloured identity" and various definition and classification of racial groups. The discussion will no doubt lead to lively and emotional debates.

However, this book is not solely about being coloured or the coloured identity or about my beliefs, my experiences or the thinking that informs my behaviour. It's really about how I can contribute and what I think my fellow compatriots should do to move our beloved country towards really embracing diversity and non-racialism. I will address the issue of racism by telling the story of my life as a coloured man and how collectively the various ethnic groups can take practical steps to engage and promote anti-racism measures in South Africa.

My hopes and prayers are that this book might make a small contribution to defeating racism. As Nelson Mandela said:

> *No one is born hating another person because of the colour of his skin, or his background or religion. People must learn to hate and if they can learn to hate they can be taught to love for love comes more naturally to the human heart than its opposite.*

Questions

1. Are you committed to non-racialism?
2. Are you setting an example to peers and family regarding respecting and promoting diversity?

Steps we can take to eradicate racism

1. Speak to your friends and colleagues from other ethnic groups to understand their lineage, culture, concerns, etc.
2. Speak to your children and let them know and understand their lineage, culture, ethnicity, struggles, etc.
3. Always discuss topical news events with your children so that they gain a broader perspective.

1. THE FUTURE

Wilma and I have three children – Jesse, Jordan, and Joshua. Joshua, our youngest son, is seven years old at the time of writing this. He attends a multiracial school, and his friends are from different racial groupings. He does not see colour but is attracted to boys and girls whose values and interests he shares. He will say, "Daddy, I don't play with Mark because he's rude," or, "I play with Carlo because he likes to play rugby." His is very confident and loyal to his friends whether they are African, white or coloured.

However, one day he came home after sports practice and told this story. The coach had to take one boy off the team, and he jokingly asked the boys who it should be. One of the white kids instantly called out, "*Die swart seun* (the black boy)."

As Josh happened to be the only boy of colour on the team, it was clear that he was being singled out as the one who should go. It could all have ended miserably for my son. However, no sooner had the white boy uttered his judgement of who should leave, the coach and the other kids raised their voices in support of Josh. "No," they said. "Josh is a good player and must stay!"

The comment by this innocent young white boy was such an eye-opener to me. Although my children attend a multiracial school and have friends of various races, there are still parents who chose to teach their children the belief system that white is better or that they must play and socialise with friends of the same racial group. However, I have met many white parents who have embraced non-racialism and are trying, as far as possible, to raise their children to embrace diversity. We as parents must proactively discuss race and identity with our children and the value of diversity.

My daughter, Jesse, has an exceptional friend called Jada. Jada happens to be a white girl, and the way Jesse speaks about her friend and the stories she shares with us reflects a young person who respects everyone and takes care to associate with peers who share her values. One day Jada wrote Jesse a poem, which I would like to share with you (with Jada's permission).

A poem to Jesse, by Jada VH

Jesse is always kind.
She is a beautiful soul and open.
She is independent and strong....
She does sport, draws and write songs.
She has a lot of talents; the list goes on & on.
I think of many pro's, but I can't think of a con.
But she sees many cons and flaws.
Right down to her core.
But if I look at her raw.
I don't see a single flaw.
I think she is beautiful, there is no debate.
I hate it when she talks badly about her looks or her weight.
So "to all the people who have hated".
You are on your own hater!
To yourself, you are a traitor.
So, stop being mean to my best friend!
I need your positivity to ascend.
I know that you don't see it.
And know it can be hard to…
But just know that I do.
If I reflect…
I think you perfect.
I hope one day, you see it too.
I hope you start loving you.
Just as much as I do.

It is inspiring to me that our children are developing meaningful relationships, even though there are many negative influences from different sectors of our society.

Albert Einstein observed that we cannot solve our problems with the same thinking we used to create them. I feel very strongly that we as the adults have an enormous responsibility not to poison our children's thinking and beliefs regarding race. They are our future, and if we want social cohesion amongst all citizens, then we as adults need to abandon our biases and racist views and must personally commit to contributing to a better life for all.

We have an enormous privilege in shaping our children's vision and moulding their character, affirming that each child is precious and possessing inherent human dignity. We, as adults, are required to teach and model the behaviour that we expect in a non-racial democratic South Africa. We must teach our children to embrace diversity and to value all human beings created in His image and likeness. Further, Christians believe in the intrinsic value of humans based in the faith in "God's creative, redemptive and consummating purpose for humankind".[5] This is at the heart of human dignity. The concept of human dignity and equality is intrinsic to combating racism, and I will expand on this concept in a later chapter.

Questions

1. Are you poisoning your child's thoughts with racist beliefs and biases?
2. Have you taught your children to value diversity?
3. Have you made a commitment to foster non-racialism with your children?

Steps you can take

1. Motivate your children to have friendships with children of various ethnic groups that share your values.
2. Set the example of how you would want your children to interact with colleagues, employees, and friends of different racial groups.
3. Try in your discussion not to stereotype any racial group but to engage with each other on a human level.

2. RACISM

Hating people because of their colour is wrong. Moreover, it doesn't matter which color does the hating. It's just plain wrong.

— *Muhammad Ali*

What is racism?

Ontario's three-year-anti-racism plan defines racism as referring to "ideas or practices that establish, maintain or perpetuate the racial superiority or dominance of one group over another." [6]

The International Convention on the Elimination of All Forms of Racial Discrimination defines racial discrimination as:

> *any distinction, exclusion, restriction or preference based on race, colour, descent, or national or ethnic origin which has the purpose or effect of nullifying or impairing the recognition, enjoyment or exercise, on an equal footing, of human rights and fundamental freedoms in the political, economic, social, cultural or any other field of public life.[7]*

Racism is not unique to South Africa but is a global problem. Fr Bryan Massingale explains in his book *Racial Injustice and the Catholic Church* that despite tireless efforts by the civil rights movement and countless other anti-racism initiatives, racism is still pervasive in America today.[8]

Renni Eddo-Lodge, a British author and journalist, explains the struggles to combat structural racism in Britain in her book *Why I'm No Longer Speaking to White People About Race*.[9]

Most Europeans viewed Africans as far back as the 1700s as inferior to white people. David Hume, a Scottish philosopher,

9

famously articulates this racist belief in his essay "Of National Characters" (1748):

> I am apt to suspect the negroes and in general all other species of men to be naturally inferior to whites. There never was a civilized nation of any other complexion than white, nor even individual eminent either in action or speculation. No ingenious manufactures, no arts no sciences.

Dr Hendrik Verwoed, the architect of apartheid, expressed a similar sentiment when he stated that the natives must be taught from young to realise that equality with the Europeans is impossible. What an ignorant view that perpetuates over the centuries to this present day.

How do we change this perception and belief system?

One way is to encourage ordinary people to tell their own stories about their experience of apartheid and racism. Friederike Bubenzer and Carolin Gomulia of the Institute for Justice and Reconciliation put it so well when they suggest that South Africa's memory archives should be "filled not only with the spectacular and the extraordinary but that ample space is created to acknowledge, remember and document the pain and suffering experienced by ordinary South Africans".[10] They affirm the view that by documenting this pain and suffering, we, as a nation, can prevent the continuation and systematic erosion of humanity as a result of 300 years of colonisation. Fr Massingale invites us to "undertake this study, despite its difficulties and risks, sustained by Christ's assurance that the truth – however painful – will indeed set us free."[11]

Dr Ruben R Richards in his book *Bastaards or Human: The Unspoken Heritage of Coloured People* states that we must "be inspired to embark on a personal journey of self-discovery, healing, restoration, and optimal living."[12]

The same approach is used by M Shawn Copeland, a Catholic theologian who uses storytelling to make people understand racial justice.[13] Copeland believes that the ugliness of racism must be exposed so that Christians will fundamentally understand the evil of racism and reject it.

Discussing racism with members of other races is awkward and can stir up emotions of anger, hatred, vengeance, unfairness and sometimes a sense of inadequacy. Inadequacy relates to African, coloured or Indian people feeling inferior in comparison with a white person. The deficiency could be described as white parents not knowing how to educate their children about the evils of apartheid or how to teach their children a new belief system where the dignity and value of each person are respected. The mountain may seem insurmountable as it might be contrary to the belief system of one's friends and family. However, we must persevere because the cancer of racism must be rooted out entirely from our society.

Apartheid has scarred all South African's in different ways, and the legacy of apartheid is still alive today. Apartheid was a racist political system. We must learn how to meaningfully engage with one another across racial divides. Most of us do not know how to meaningfully participate with colleagues and friends of different ethnic groups, especially the boys and girls that grew up in segregated communities during apartheid. Having been socialised in one-race communities, Africans, coloureds, Indians and whites mostly still live in their isolated and homogenous communities. We went to schools with one racial group, partied with friends of the same ethnic group, married partners of the same ethnic group and prayed and worshipped with people of the same ethnic group. Yes, there were exceptions, but in no small extent, this was our socialisation.

As a result of living in the various segregated communities, all racial groups developed certain biases and stereotypes. Each has their derogatory words or descriptions of other ethnic groups. Even the Africans have derogatory terms for coloured people as explained by Brenda Wardle in her book *Coloured Diaries: Experiences of an Eastern Cape 'Mixed Breed'* where she describes being referred to us as *amaLawu, amaQheya* or *amaQhakancu*.[14] So yes, we all have been scarred by apartheid. However, all South Africans must confront their family, friends or peers when derogatory terms are used to refer to any racial group. We must eliminate these terms from our vocabulary.

Questions

1. Are you allowing derogatory terms referring to other racial groups to be used in your presence?
2. What are you doing to teach your children regarding their specific identity?
3. Are you open to engaging with all South Africans regarding your beliefs?

Steps you can take

1. Share your personal story.
2. Be brave and write the story of your own experiences and beliefs growing up in South Africa. Your story is important!

3. MY OWN BIAS

Watch your thoughts; they become words.
Watch your words; they become actions.
Watch your actions; they become habits.
Watch your habits; they become character.
Watch your character; it becomes your destiny.

—*Frank Outlaw, actor*

In the early days of the European settlement at the Cape the young Dutch men were attracted to the local Khoisan and slave women and had relationships with them. Some of these women had children with these Dutch men, and this was the start of a community that was steeped in both European, African and Indonesian cultures.

A prominent example of the relationships that existed between Dutch and Khoi is the marriage between Dr Pieter van Meerhof, the Chief Medical Officer of the Dutch East India Company at the Cape, and Krotoa in 1664.[15] Their children contributed to what we now called the coloured population.

The children of these mixed-race couples had a world view that incorporated the perspectives of the Dutch as well as those of the local population. However, gradually negative connotations started to develop around this mixed-race heritage. One of the arguments was that two so-called pure races had been diluted to form a new mixed race, and this mixture was somehow inferior.

Nowadays we can see this for the rubbish it is. What on earth is a pure race? The history of humanity is a story of constant mixing and cross-pollination. Without it our species would be dead!

The term "coloured" is a contentious issue among a portion of the coloured population. This part of the coloured community believes coloured people should be referred to as Africans as it links us to the land. The land in South Africa has become a political hot potato as, at the time of writing, politicians are conducting public hearings relating to the expropriation of land without compensation in all corners of South Africa. The Khoisan descendants were systematically stripped of their identity and disposed of their land.

The aim of the Dutch, Boers and later the British was to strip these mixed-race communities of their identity to create a submissive and obedient working class for the white masters. The entrepreneurial spirit was destroyed, and instead, they were encouraged to become manual labourers and artisans to support the white masters' business interests.

Our colonial and apartheid socialisation has a severe negative impact on our identity as a coloured community. Over the last 400 years, it has resulted in biases amongst all races about other races that are not their own. When reflecting on some of my thoughts and beliefs, I know that my socialisation has resulted in me having a muddied viewpoint. I remember a story my mother told us. The classification of my maternal grandmother as coloured and her siblings as white. When my mom retold this aspect of our family history, it was from the perspective that Ma's sister and brothers were white and therefore, by implication, somewhere out there we had a white family. But none of my mother's siblings spoke about our African heritage because for Ma to come out a bit darker with not-so-straight hair meant that we had African ancestry. However, we were silent on this aspect of our history.

Why?

During the 1970s, Afrikaans genealogist JA Heese found records indicating that more than 1,200 European men in South Africa married non-white women between 1652 and 1800.[16] Extrapolating this information revealed that approximately 7.2% of Afrikaner heritage was non-white. The apartheid regime conveniently neglected to inform the rest of the Afrikaners.

The apartheid regime created an absurd and laughable system where individuals could manoeuver to "improve" their individual racial identity and classification, provided they were not discovered to be a fraud. Therefore, coloured people could be classified as white and Africans could become coloured.

Max du Preez in his prologue to Brenda Wardle's book *Coloured Diaries*, notes that "we're a mixed masala, like few other nations"[17] and refers to scientific research that found that white South Africans who are so obsessed with pure European blood have at least 7% "Black" blood. In this light, the majority of South Africans should have been classified as coloured by the apartheid regime.

So, Ma's experience was not unique! There are thousands of people who were classified white but had mixed heritage. The destruction or collapse of many families because of the racial classification was partly due to some siblings betraying their brothers or sisters who had darker skin. They merely cut that brother or sister off and had no further contact with them. They were scared that if the government found out that they had a mixed-race heritage that would lose their privileges of being classified white.

But I am dodging the question about why we individually and collectively as a family do not consider our African (Khoisan) heritage. Could it be that it was not convenient? Could it be that our socialisation created a racist belief that having a potential white family was better?

As you grow from a child into an adult, you have a duty to yourself to challenge your beliefs and socialised bias. You cannot keep blaming your parents for your racist views or your mistaken sense of identity.

Questions

1. Are you challenging your beliefs and personal biases?
2. Have you learned how to identify your own hidden bias?
3. Are you continually trying to understand other people's identity, beliefs, and history?
4. Are you open to engage with and form meaningful friendships with people of other racial groups?
5. Are you speaking out against racism?

Steps you can take

1. Spend time understanding and reflecting on your beliefs.
2. Compare your thoughts and ideas to a universally accepted objective standard, e.g. religious teaching, human rights law.
3. Correct your beliefs if they are wrong.

4. A BRIEF OVERVIEW OF SOUTH AFRICA

We, the people of South Africa,
Recognise the injustices of the past;
Honour those who suffered for justice and freedom in our
land;
Respect those who have worked to build and develop our
country; and
Believe that South Africa belongs to all who live in it,
united in diversity.

—Preamble, South African Constitution

A skewed version of history was taught at schools during the apartheid era. The history focused on the advancements of white people and left out large sections of the history of the indigenous people. Today we are still struggling to obtain the right balance regarding the historical content and outcomes that we expect young South Africans to learn. For the coloured people, large tracks of our history have been abandoned by the white man to strip us of our identity, and we must research and once again educate ourselves and our children about our ancestry.

I want to venture to say that part of the problem why the coloured communities are in such turmoil is that we do not know our history and therefore do not have an understanding and comprehension of what the vision for us is in a democratic South Africa. And because we do not see the idea we do not know what we must do now to take strides to achieve that vision.

The shores of Cape Town have seen Asian and European ships from the 15th century. Here they found the San who were hunter-gatherers and the Khoe who were crop growers and sheepherders. These two tribes are now usually referred to as the Khoisan.[18] The

17

area they lived in stretched from the Northern Cape to the Cape Town and all the way to Port Elizabeth. Sailors stayed in the Cape for a different period, which could have been for several months.[19] They engaged with the indigenous populations, and their impact on the South African psyche and communities is still felt today. The narrative that the mixed-race communities started after 1652 is false.[20] In the early 1600s until the arrival of Jan van Riebeek, various African, Asian and European sailors visited the Cape and engaged with the indigenous populations and had intimate relationships with the local women.[21] The indigenous population was entrepreneurial as they initially provided services such as stevedoring and trading for these sailors.[22] However, with the arrival of Jan van Riebeek, the indigenous population was forced out, and the Dutch took over these activities. Some of the indigenous groups, like the Khoena, were forced into servitude while the San were almost completely obliterated.[23]

Similar to the Khoena, the Griquas suffered injustice in their interaction with white settlers. The communities imploded because of the distribution of alcohol, tobacco and trade with copper plates. Local women also traded with their bodies for material rewards from these sailors. The numbers of offspring from white men and local women grew exponentially. Not all of the sexual relationships that these women had was consensual. One of the stories is of the Griqua people. A local Griqua girl by the name of Francine was the offspring of a white farmer and an indentured slave. She was raped by a farmer's son at the age of 14.[24] Once the settler family found out about the pregnancy, they kicked Francine off the farm. Another farmer, named Adam Tas, took pity on her circumstances and took her to his farm. She gave birth to a boy child, and she called him Adam Eta. Later in his life, a white man changed Adam's surname from Eta to Kok. Kok was an indication of Adam's occupation, namely that of a chef.

The breakup of the Khoikhoi was already underway when the white people arrived in the Cape. The breakup according to the study was because of lousy leadership and the nomadic lifestyle of the Khoikhoi.

The officials of the Dutch East India company traded with the Khoikhoi, especially for meat. Later, because of unsustainable trade, the Khoikhoi lost their livelihood and became servants of the white people. The Khoikhoi disintegrated slowly socially and economically. Further, the Khoikhoi met different ethnic groups stationed at the Cape. They formed friendships with these ethnic groups and some developed into intimate relationships with the slave, Dutchmen, renegade sailors and other indigenous people.

One of the family groups that had a mixed heritage was the Afrikaner-Oorlams whose lineage was mainly from the Khoikhoi and slaves.[25] As a result of the Khoikhoi disintegration, the Afrikaner-Oorlams left the farming lifestyle. This decision was made by Klaas Afrikaner, the leader of the Afrikaner-Oorlams. They were taught by the Dutch to ride horses and to shoot. With these skills, they were used as hunters and trackers. The Oorlams abandoned their Khoikhoi structure, livelihood and culture and became westernised, dressing like Europeans and speaking Cape Hollands. Later, the Afrikaner-Oorlams leader, Jager Afrikaner, son of Klaas, made the decision for the group to leave the service of the Dutch.

When Jager died, his son Jonker took over the leadership and the group dominated the Northern Cape and the region known today as Namibia. This was as a result of Jonker's strategic direction and diplomatic competence, as well as the group's expertise in the use of weapons. Jonker also formed strategic alliances that advantaged the group.

The other group that I want to mention was the Basters. Their lineage was Khoikhoi who had relationships with slaves and whites.[26] Many clashes took place between Basters and Afrikaner-Oorlams. On many occasions they were used in opposition to each other to further the agenda of the colonists. However, all these mixed-race groups had an influence on what today is the coloured community. All these groups were used by the colonisers when it was convenient but were regarded by them as being inferior.

Further, since the arrival of Jan van Riebeek in 1652, South Africa has struggled with racism. Racism has its foundation in the arrival of the Dutch, who believed that the indigenous people they encountered were inferior to them in all aspects including physically, intellectually, emotionally and morally.[27] Later, the Boer people started to develop a separate identity and belief system. Slowly the Boers became their own nation and their relationship with the Netherlands began to disintegrate. Expatriate Dutch viewed the Boers as lazy, corrupt, narrow-minded and incompetent.[28] They were ashamed of their distant relatives. It is strange that this view is today held by some white (Boer/Afrikaner people) about black people.

Similarly, the British, who occupied the Cape from 1815 onwards, believed themselves to be the greatest and most civilised nation that the world has seen.[29] They further thought that they had a sacred mission to attain worldwide perfection by dominating and controlling other countries.

This belief system has continued to exist from generation to generation among some white people. Meaning some white children have inherited a skewed belief system from their parents. Further, the apartheid regime perpetuated the idea of white supremacy. The foundation of apartheid was racial classification.[30] Today this is aptly illustrated when you visit the Apartheid Museum in Johannesburg. The apartheid government classified South Africans into one of four groups, namely native, coloured, Asian and white. With being white came immense privileges. These privileges included a higher percentage of spending on health care and education. In the financial year 1975/76 the apartheid state spent R644 per year on each white pupil, R189 on each Indian pupil, R139 on each coloured pupil, and only R42 on each African pupil.[31] This had a significant impact on the quality of education, literacy and later employability of blacks who grew up during apartheid. It is just logical that white people had a better chance of developing academic and business skills because of the funding and exposure they received.

This skewed allocation in favour of white people in South Africa meant whites could afford good healthcare and nutritious food, while blacks were left with an inferior health system and an inability to afford adequate nutrition. This resulted in lower life expectancy, higher infant mortality rates and generally lower quality of life for blacks

The apartheid regime further assisted white-owned businesses to succeed. Legislation was developed to divide certain occupations among the different segments of the white population. For instance, business opportunities for Jewish people were curtailed to advance other sections of the white community. Africans, coloureds and Indians had no chance to trade or do business with the white people.

Also, the apartheid government created organisations such as Transnet and Iscor to provide work for white men and women. Senior positions in companies were reserved for white men. White people were empowered economically. Thus, over the last few decades, white people had the opportunity to create wealth and abundance for their families. The majority of Africans, and to a lesser extent coloureds and Indians, lived in poverty. That why we speak about racialised inequality.

It is ingenious now of white people to want decisions on employability to be taken on merit. Yes, some blacks can compete on an equal basis due to them putting in a significant amount of effort and sacrifice to gain the skills and competencies to compete on a merit basis. However, many black people were not given the opportunity, the funds, the academic support and business exposure to develop their skills and competencies. So we should invest in these communities to provide them with these skills and competencies and then allow appointments to be made on merit only. Although there are some black people in the position to compete, a significant portion of these communities need socio-economic and political assistance to fully develop this latent potential.

The Employment Equity Act is a swear word for most white people; however, it is a logical vehicle to ensure black people attain the skills and competencies required to compete on an equal footing with white people. Substantive equality tries to correct the economic imbalance that has been created because of years of white privilege and wealth creation.

However, I do believe that there should be a time limit on all affirmative action measures. Affirmative action is not a permanent crutch to be used – it is meant to be more like an ankle brace that you use until your foot is healed and you can carry your own body weight.

Or maybe the late professor Sampie Terblanche's idea is more feasible. He argued that more should be done to achieve a better understanding of the systemic injustices that occurred in South Africa. He stated that white people should undergo adult education to educate them about the true nature of the horrors, exploitation and injustices of the twentieth century. Without this education, reconciliation will not be durable. He further argues that white people need to confess and show the necessary repentance in order to achieve conversion, and this requires sacrifice.[32]

Professor Terblanche also advocated for the implementation of a wealth tax but received robust criticism from a business-orientated newspaper. However, I do believe a combination of Professor Terblanche's two arguments for a defined period could be a durable solution.

I have seen in many industries that white men have dragged their feet in implementing affirmative action and other transformation policies. This only prolongs the pain and heightens the aggression and anxiety of previously disadvantaged people. The apartheid regime knew precisely what they were doing and the consequences of their actions. As Dr Verwoerd stated, the apartheid policies and the oppression of blacks, in general, will cause black people to increasingly develop a sense of resentment and revenge. However, most African, coloured and Indian people are committed to the ongoing reconciliation process amongst all racial groups. But part of the ongoing reconciliation and social cohesion process is economic transformation.

However, I do believe that the new generation of "born free" children should be given hope and the space to develop to their full potential. But we need to ensure that the socio-economic rights of all born-free black children are attained, especially ensuring that they receive the best education possible.

Questions

1. Are you resisting economic transformation taking place in South Africa?
2. Are you an advocate for meaningful participation of all South African in the economy?
3. Do you understand Section 28 of the Constitution?

Steps you can take

1. Acknowledgement by white South Africans that apartheid created a legacy of problems we are still dealing with.
2. Acknowledgement by white South Africans that their families and communities unfairly benefited during apartheid, resulting in the unfair economic position experienced today.
3. Once a problem is admitted to and owned then we can develop pragmatic solutions.
4. Black South Africans must continue to uplift a broader spectrum of people with skills and competencies to take up the required roles and responsibilities in society.

5. SOUTH AFRICAN GIFTS TO THE WORLD

None of us comes into the world fully formed. We would not know how to think, or walk, or speak, or behave as human beings unless we learned it from other human beings. We need other human beings in order to be human.

—*Archbishop Desmond Tutu*

South Africa received praise for its peaceful transition from apartheid to a democratic dispensation. Also, South Africa has given the world three additional gifts that we can be immensely proud of, namely the Truth and Reconciliation process, the practice of ubuntu and the progressive Constitution.

Truth and Reconciliation Commission (TRC)

At the dawn of the new democratic dispensation, the new South African parliament promulgated the Promotion of National Unity and Reconciliation Act, No 34 of 1995. In the words of the Minister of Justice at that time, Dullar Omar, "the commission is a necessary exercise to enable South Africans to come to terms with their past on a morally accepted basis and to advance the cause of reconciliation".[33]

I remember being glued to the television watching victims appearing at TRC hearings seeking answers about what happened to their loved ones. They wanted to know when and how their loved ones died and who was responsible for their deaths. Although many families had the opportunity to confront some of the perpetrators, they have never found complete closure. There are millions of people that have not been able to tell their stories or to engage with white people regarding their indignities, torture, loss, and humiliation suffered. This resentment of not being

24

provided with this opportunity contributes to the racial tension that exists today in South Africa. We need to implement programmes and platforms for this engagement to happen and for ordinary people to tell their stories and find closure.

After the TRC, the Gallows Exhumation Project, led by the Missing Person's Task Team, commenced its work. They are still today, 25 years after the dawn of democracy, searching for the remains of political prisoners who were executed by the apartheid government. The Gallows project is an important task because it helps families find out how their loved ones died and where they are buried, finally bringing a sense of closure and the possibility of reconciliation.

Yes, the TRC had its flaws; however, South Africa has given the world a vehicle to use after conflict situations to find some form of justice and reconciliation.

Ubuntu

Ubuntu is an African philosophical concept. Ubuntu can be defined as a characteristic that comprises the essential human virtues of compassion and humanity. The African philosophy is an approach to community and life and manifests itself in a code of behaviour. Ubuntu, in my opinion, has become popular amongst non-Africans because of media attention and because people like a term that is simple and easy to understand. However, in the new democratic dispensation, ubuntu is also closely linked to the South African Constitutional value of human dignity. The virtues of compassion and humanity also manifest in the protection, promotion and respect for human rights in general. In my opinion, the compassion and humanity of the community should also find expression in the minimal level of socio-economic rights of the community. The concept of socio-economic rights will be explored later in this book. Both Desmond Tutu and Nelson Mandela were strong advocates of the concept and practice of ubuntu.

However, I am not sure if the concept is understood and practised widely in South Africa. I can only speak of my experience living in coloured communities. Although the coloured communities had compassion and humanity we did not relate this to the African philosophical concept of ubuntu.

More should be done by civil society and the government to educate all South African's about the concept of ubuntu and have practical plans for how we can promote and practise ubuntu in our respective local communities. The practice and education of the principles of ubuntu can be a foundational building block to combat racism and launch various anti-racism projects.

The South African Constitution

The South African Constitution is a progressive document. Section 1 of the Constitution places human dignity, the achievement of equality, and the advancement of human rights and freedoms as fundamental to the new democratic dispensation.[34]

Section 10 the Constitution states: "Everyone has inherent dignity and the right to have their dignity respected and protected."

Human dignity is a fundamental value as it originates firstly from respect for oneself, and secondly, from the recognition that all human beings have absolute value just because of being human. Racism attacks this fundamental value of our Constitution, and we should continually take steps to defeat racism at all cost.

Further, Section 9 of the Constitution contains the equality clause which prohibits unfair discrimination while providing legislative and other measures to achieve substantive equality, address systemic discrimination and eradicate social and economic inequalities.

The equality clause must be interpreted within the historical context of South Africa.[35] The interpretation must take into account the past injustices and lived experiences of South Africans during apartheid and the type of country the Constitution envisions as articulated in the preamble. During apartheid, the white minority were advantaged in terms of receiving a disproportionate amount of the country's resources while the African, coloured and Indian people received much less.

Some of the legislative proposals that the South African government has implemented to remedy these inequalities are the Promotion of Equality and the Prevention of Unfair

Discrimination Act, the Employment Equity Act and the Broad-Based Black Economic Empowerment Act. At the time of writing, the South African Parliament is undertaking public debate about whether to expropriate land without compensation to restore the property to their rightful owners. Serious discussions continue, and the descendants of the Korana, Khoi, Griqua and San people believing they are the rightful owners, and African people thinking they are the rightful owners. The debate continues. However, the Constitution provides a process and mechanism for the resolution of these conflicts.

These conflicts have, however, evoked frustration, anxiety and even hate by some members of South African society.

Questions

5. Do you have a copy of the South African Constitution?
6. Do you understand the constitutional provisions relating to dignity, freedom, and equality, the foundational values of the South African Constitution?
7. Does your behaviour promote and protect the dignity, freedom, and equality of fellow South Africans?
8. Are you resisting significant transformation and redress?

Steps you can take

1. Read books and articles dealing with the concepts of human dignity and of the African philosophical concept of ubuntu.
2. Regularly read the South African Constitution.

6. MY STORY

*It's time to take your stories and solutions and transform
them into action.*

—Michael Coteau,
Canada Minister Responsible for Anti-Racism

I was born on a cold winter's day in my paternal grandmother's
house in the small coloured township of Bonteheuwel on the
outskirts of Cape Town in South Africa. The Bonteheuwel
community is a product of the segregation policies and legislation
of the apartheid regime.

Initially, many of the coloured residents in Cape Town lived
near the city centre in a suburb known as District Six, but many
also lived in the southern suburbs such as Claremont and
Rondebosch. The removal of my parents and grandparents from
these communities to Bonteheuwel and other Cape Flats
communities situated 25 kilometres and more from the city centre
created a massive disruption to their lives. These townships had
limited infrastructure and no or minimal recreational facilities.
Bonteheuwel was a desolate and impoverished population. The
Cape Flats, an expansive, flat, sandy area far from the mountain
and business areas became known as apartheid's dumping ground.

Over the last 30 years, the Cape Flats communities have
become infested with gangs and riven with drug abuse. Addiction
to tik (crystal meth) is an epidemic. In some families, the parents
and children are all tik addicts. Projections put the gang-related
murders in Bonteheuwel for 2019 at more than 80 people, most of
whom would be young people.

Bonteheuwel's socio-economic problems persist and have a
devastating effect on the lives of children growing up in these

communities. However, many devout Christians and Muslims are living in the area and are having a positive influence. I grew up in a home where we were taught to be thankful for our blessings, however small, to respect everyone and to obey the Commandments.

During apartheid, and I would suggest still today, Bonteheuwel residents suffered various human rights violations. In the 1980s the population stood at around 45,000 people. All of us were poor. Education was substandard. A few young sons and daughters of Bonteheuwel's community paid the highest sacrifice for the liberation of all black people, while others were beaten and tortured. I remember especially people like Christopher Truter, an Arcadia Senior Secondary School pupil who was shot dead when police opened fire into a crowd of protesting pupils. I remember Ashley Kriel, a young Bonteheuwel activist killed by the police in 1987 in Athlone, and Coline Williams, a daughter of Bonteheuewel who sacrificed her life along with other comrades so that we can enjoy the privileges we have today. I salute these young men and women, and their sacrifice should never be forgotten.

Out of the coloured community came prominent leaders in the anti-apartheid struggle such as Alan Boesak. He led many anti-apartheid initiatives against the apartheid regime.

Alan stated in a public theology lecture that in the 1980s, imprisonment and torture were rife, and that anti-apartheid activists were notoriously frightened of places like John Vorster Square, Pollsmoor Prison, and Vlakplaas. Boesak stated that he had seen cruelty that he could not imagine and still cannot forget and that the media attention showed the world that a crime against humanity had been committed.[36]

Why I recall these South African's events in the coloured community and other black communities is to remind all about the enormous sacrifice that members of the coloured community have made. The victors normally restate history, but for South Africa to move forward, history must be retold in an honest, balanced and fair manner acknowledging the contributions in the anti-apartheid movement by members of the African, coloured, Indian and white communities. But we must also be forthright in recognising how the various racial groups perpetuate racism.

One of the adverse and hidden effects of our formation during the apartheid legacy is our limiting beliefs as a people. We do not live lives that reflect the powerful testimony that in each of us lies untapped potential, creativity, and blessings. We have been raised to believe that we are not worthy of success or material abundance. A good example is when some coloured people buy a new TV, phone or electrical appliance and they do not understand how the appliance works, so they will say, "I don't understand how this white man's stuff works." Is this not a limiting belief?

I think the saddest legacy of apartheid is that parents in 2019, 25 years after the birth of democracy, still feel the need to poison their children's minds with racist biases. Some white parents are still perpetuating this notion of white supremacy. What an injustice you are doing to your child. However, African and coloured parents must raise their children to believe that within them lies untapped potential, creativity, and blessings.

Today I live in the predominately affluent community of Eversdal, Durbanville, in Cape Town. I married Wilma, who grew up in the northern suburbs of Cape Town and our children Jesse, Jordan, and Joshua attend Model C public schools in the area. The Model C school is a semi-private school structure that provides a better education than the traditional public township schools. The location of Model C schools is predominately in wealthier communities, and some Model C schools have prestigious histories dating back many years. However, these schools are predominately white (both from a learner population and educators' perspective). Most of the coloured and African community cannot afford to send their children to Model C schools. Children attending these schools have access to good infrastructure, good sports coaching, committed teachers, etc. In most township schools this is lacking.

I am the second eldest child of Maureen and Andrew. During our early childhood years, my mom was a machinist in a clothing factory; however, later she became a full-time mom. My father was a storeman, but there were long episodes when he was unemployed or suffered from depression which required hospitalisation.

My mom was a significant positive force in nurturing us as children, and both parents instilled Christian values. The Christian values included respect for women, treating people fairly and having a strong worth ethic. My mom created a vision for her children to complete high school and to study further. This was somewhat unusual for Bonteheuwel, where many of my peers were not encouraged to finish high school or even to aspire to anything more than blue-collar work once they'd made it through matric.

This approach by my mom aligns with the findings of psychologist Emmy Werner, who conducted a 40-year study into the critical ingredients for children to thrive and be successful even though they came from impoverished backgrounds.[37] She stated that there are three ingredients children must have:

- A strong bond with a supportive caregiver or teacher.
- The ability to act autonomously and independently, meeting the world head-on.
- The possession of self-control and a belief that hard work, rather than their environment, will determine their future.

I have explained that my mother fulfilled their first requirement. I have always been a diligent student. I passed grade 8 at Rosewood Primary in Bonteheuwel as the top student. I spent a year at a local High School and then decided that I wanted to go to a better school. My maternal grandfather and I then went to various schools in the Athlone area looking for a new school for me. We managed to obtain a place at Athlone High. I passed grade 12 in 1991 and went on to study accounting for three years at Peninsula Technikon, today known as Cape Peninsula University of Technology. After the initial studies, I further completed business and legal degrees at distance learning universities and was admitted to several professional associations. I have recently passed my doctorate degree.

So yes, I can confirm through personal experience that the study of Emmy Werner is correct. The study provides a good guideline for parents, communities, civil society and churches to focus on in nurturing well-balanced boys and girls in these impoverished communities.

Questions

1. What is your personal story?
2. Have you shared your story with people of other racial groups?

Steps you can take

1. Tell your story.
2. Civil society should have programmes that teach parent about the critical elements required to raise well-balanced adults as articulated by Emmy Werner.
3. Implement systematic, robust interventions to eradicate drugs from the Cape Flats.

7. COLOURISM

Colourism is the prejudice, discrimination or undervaluing of people with dark skin tone and the appreciation or valuing of people with lighter skin tone, typically among people of the same ethnic or racial group. The coloured community has practised colourism for years. The coloured population, because of its mixed heritage, has people that look like Africans and some who look like white people, with the full spectrum in-between. The whiter you look, the more favourable and attractive society deems you. This subtle racism in the coloured community existed when I was young but still exists today. The practice can hurt a person's self-esteem and self-worth. Of my siblings, I am relatively dark in complexion while my older brother is more fair with lighter coloured hair. The contrast was even more noticeable when we were younger. We were called e'Lollipop after a favourite movie about a white boy and an African boy who were friends. I was the "African boy" and my brother the "white boy".

When strangers saw my mom's children they would ask in Afrikaans, "*is daai swartjie joune?* (is that black boy yours?)"

My mom on a few occasions told of how African women would frequently come into the coloured communities to look for old clothes. I recall an incident that my mother retold of an African woman who asked that I be given to them to be taken to Transkei. While growing up, I was regularly teased about my dark complexion and was called names such as "kaffir poppie" or "kef".

If you do not have self-belief and vision for yourself, these uninvited and stupid comments and labels that family and peers give you will become a stumbling block and will negatively affect your psyche, confidence and relationships in the future.

In my teenage years, girls with light complexion, straight hair and green or hazel eyes received much of the attention. If a girl was dark and had coarse hair, she received very little attention. Pathetic! This practice continues amongst a portion of the coloured population and is completely unacceptable. Today we should teach our boys and girls to appreciate and value people with good manners, morally correct conduct, academic diligence and participation in sport and cultural activities. Coloured children should definitely be actively discouraged from practising colourism.

We should not allow or encourage our children to value superficial and/or material attributes or things that do nothing to uplift or affirm every person dignity and inherent self-worth.

If we do continue with the practice of colourism, remember you are complicit in advancing the narrative that white people are better than black people.

Questions

1. Do you have nicknames for friends and family members that refer to their dark-skinned complexion?
2. Are you still teaching your children to value their friends' features as opposed to their values and conduct?
3. Are you encouraging all girls to believe that they can be anything they want to be and do not need a boy/man to affirm their importance?

Steps we can take

1. Stop giving nicknames to friends and family members that reflect their dark-skinned complexion.
2. The educational curriculum of South Africa must address the issue of colourism in the Life Orientation subject at school.

8. MY ROLE IN COMBATTING RACISM

The equal participation of all individuals and peoples in the formation of just, equitable, democratic and inclusive societies can contribute to a world free from racism.

—*World Conference Against Racism, Racial Discrimination, Xenophobia, and Related Intolerance*

My primary role is to educate myself regarding racism, intolerance, and discrimination. I have been a habitual student for the last 27 years. I believe in lifelong learning. One of the exciting and impactful non-academic courses I was fortunate to attend was the Gordon Institute of Business Science (GIBS) Nexus programme. In 2008, I was working for Exxaro in Pretoria as a Strategic Sourcing Manager, and they funded me to go on the course. The course involved young leaders from business, civil society, and government meeting every week to be exposed to experiential initiatives, followed by group discussions on the experiences.

The Nexus programme focused on five core areas, namely dialogue, deepening contextual understanding, authenticity, agency, and vision.

The participants from various racial groups engaged in tough and uncomfortable conversations about race and racial justice. We shared our personal experiences of the crimes that took place during apartheid. The engagements were usually after our experiential outings. These experiential outings attempted to deepen our contextual understanding of certain political and historically significant events in our country. We had experienced facilitators who took us to the Apartheid Museum, Liliesleaf Farm, Vlakplaas, the Voortrekker Monument and Freedom Park.

The two places that had the most significant impact on me was the Voortrekker Monument and Vlakplaas.

Vlakplaas is situated about 20 km outside the city of Pretoria and was the headquarters of the apartheid government's 15-member death squad. This death squad was an elite operational unit of assassins under the Security Police. At Vlakplaas, Jaques Pauw, one of South Africa's best-known investigative journalists, informed the group of the atrocities that happened there. Incidents where anti-apartheid activists were abducted, tortured and burnt next to the braai where security police were cooking their meat. Pauw explained how the police were assisted by askaris – former anti-apartheid activists who had been turned and now helped in the abduction, torture, and murder of anti-apartheid activists. Pauw investigated these atrocities committed by the security police but, more importantly, interviewed Eugene De Kock, one of the most ruthless perpetrators of violence and torture against anti-apartheid activists. The visit to Vlakplaas exposed us to the horrors of apartheid and to the extent that the apartheid regime was willing to go to maintain white privilege.

The other Nexus visit that made an impact on me was the one to the Voortrekker Monument. The monument was built by descendants of the Voortrekkers to honour God. I know that there is a very contentious history of the Battle of Blood River. Later in the history of South Africa, our people we imprisoned, tortured, murdered and our families were destroyed by the descendants of the Voortrekkers. Further, there were white Christians and certain Christian churches which were complicit in promoting and implementing the atrocious propaganda and policies of the apartheid regime.

However, as a Christian I could relate to the Voortrekkers' cry to our God and that they kept their promise to honour God. The Voortrekkers, in their hour of need, had that honest engagement with God in terms of what they required and what they would do if God's promise was fulfilled. They kept their promise and built an authentic symbol of that covenantal promise in the form of the Voortrekker monument. The behaviour that most impressed me was the integrity that they had after receiving the blessing of their lives to come back and honour God in this way. This is a true story of the love and faith between God and his faithful.

Another moment in me improving my understanding of racism was my participation at the Winter Living Theology seminar in July 2018, organised by the Jesuit Institute of South Africa. Fr Bryan Massingale gave a series of lectures about racial justice and the demands of discipleship. My main take-away from the two days of lectures and discussions was that although the Catholic Church has acknowledged racism, there have been leaders and church institutions that have perpetuated it. Everyone has a moral duty to confront racism and racists institutions, both secular and religious.

Questions

1. Are you telling demeaning jokes and stories of people of other races?
2. Are you making an effort to gain a more holistic understanding of South African history?
3. Do you tacitly condone racism by your conduct when you do not challenge racist comments?
4. How can you become a strong advocate for non-racialism and diversity?

9. MY ROLE AS A PARENT IN COMBATTING RACISM

Your kids watch you for a living. It's their job; it's what they do. That's why it is so important to try your best to be a good role model.

—*James Lehman*

We cannot raise our children in current South Africa to believe that we all require the same treatment. We need to teach our white children that most black children (coloured, Indian and African) are not starting from the same favourable position as most white children.

We need to raise white children to understand that there are black children that have substantial hurdles to overcome and might require more assistance to achieve significant equality. However, there are black children who are not disadvantaged and must compete on merit.

These are not easy discussions to have. It is difficult for white parents to teach their children to treat all children as equals while at the same time saying that black children need more assistance and must be treated differently. The aim is to make white children aware of the situation without burdening them with guilt. All parents want their children to have healthy self-esteem and self-worth, and the issues of race and racial justice must be done in a loving and caring environment.

I am a Christian, and if I were attempting to discuss the issues with my child, I would approach it from the perspective of love. We are all called to love one another and love entails sharing, caring and wanting the best for all children. Therefore, we must care for the most vulnerable children in our communities and our country.

As parents, we must develop within our children a healthy and correct understanding of how we relate to other races. The ideal would be that all children are treated equally and that all South African have a similar outlook on race relations. We know this is not the case. We as parents need to be at the forefront of having conversations with our children. Failure will result in their perspectives and beliefs being formed by family, friends, the media and other influencers – some of whom might not be providing appropriate input into your child's healthy development.

I also feel very strongly that we, as black parents, should recognise when our children have received sufficient material support (especially for Model C school pupils) to enable them to compete on merit for any position. Rightfully or wrongfully this is what I am teaching Jesse, Jordan, and Joshua. Yes, when I see educators and coaches having racist tendencies I will address these, but my children have been provided with a loving home and a supportive environment, and their material and educational needs have been met. They must productively contribute to South Africa, and they must assist with the upliftment of vulnerable groups. *They are not disadvantaged.*

Questions

1. What sort of person do you want your child to become?
2. Have you discussed this with your child?
3. Is your child being exposed to groups, people and institutions that will have a positive impact on their character?
4. What are the subtle messages that your actions and behaviour are teaching your child?

Steps you can take

1. Teach your children to value diversity.
2. Teach your children to respect, value, and promote the right of all to their culture, language and heritage, provided it conforms with the South African Constitution.

10. OUR COLLECTIVE ROLE AS THE COLOURED COMMUNITY

The great courageous act that we must all do, is to step out
of our history and past so that we can live our dreams.

—*Oprah Winfrey*

The word "coloured" describes a community of people whose identity was moulded during the apartheid era. Today, studies have revealed that the coloured population has a diverse ancestry including European, African, Asian and Khoisan. The Cape Town coloureds have a diverse lineage that comprises overwhelmingly Khoisan and African lineage and to a lesser extent a European and Asian lineage.[38] The racist apartheid regime classified coloured people based on specific criteria and forced them through the Group Areas Act to live in defined residential areas and attend schools and worship within a geographical community.[39] This community developed a mindset of removal or separateness from other races in South Africa.

Some sections of the coloured community view the term "coloured" as offensive and hold the view that coloured people should be referred to by the different tribes such as Khoi, San, Griqua, Khorana and the Nama. Many coloured people do not know the tribe from which their ancestry originates. The lack of knowledge is partly caused by the absence of effective leadership in the community. There is also not enough engagement with the entire coloured community regarding how they would like the matter addressed.

I understand that globally the term "coloured" is offensive, but for many coloured people the term is owned with pride. This is how I see it. I am proudly coloured. My community/ethnic group has one of the most diverse ancestries in the world. I am proud of the township from which I came, namely Bonteheuwel. I am proud of the many contributions made by coloured people. Why must I be ashamed of my community and my history?

Yes, I hear the arguments that coloured is an apartheid construct. I hear the case that the word "coloured" is scientifically and culturally incorrect! I understand the evidence that colonialism has given us a false sense of race, but I celebrate my history and the community that formed and made me the person I am today. I praise the use of the word "coloured", and if coloured people have a problem, let us unite and engage meaningfully about what we want to be called. No one is going to dictate what I should be called.

When I refer to coloured people, it is people who were socialised and raised within these so-called coloured communities. These are the places, events and people my family and I shared our lives with. Although we, as mixed-race communities, can trace our lineage back 500 years, I am referring to socialised and lived experiences in these coloured communities. They experienced the struggles and joys of living in these communities. In September and October 2018, violent protests took place in the coloured communities of Bonteheuwel, Bishop Lavis, Westbury, and Eldorado Park. These coloured communities felt that the provincial and national governments had neglected them, resulting in many socio-economic challenges such as gangsterism, drug epidemics, teenage pregnancy, high unemployment, femicide, and domestic violence. I empathise with these communities.

Although most of the socio-economic problems mentioned above also affect African communities, they affect coloured communities in a disproportionate way. In the years from 1991 to 2006, coloured matriculants had a 53.5% increase from 22 405 to 34 417.[40] However, the matriculants who passed with matric exemptions decreased from 22% to 17%. This is an indictment if you consider that matric exemption increases one's chances for employment and further educational opportunities.

The coloured population is approximately 8.8% of the entire South African society.[41] A national study undertaken in 2004 on female homicide revealed some startling results. For instance, the

41

risk of coloured women being killed by an intimate partner was 18.3 per 100 000, while for African women it was 8.9, Indian women 7.5, and white women 2.8.[42]

Similarly, the number of coloured men and women in prison is about 18.5%. This is significantly higher the other ethnic groups and has a detrimental effect on the community and on boys that grow up without a father or mother figure.

Many of these challenges have their genesis in apartheid policies, but we can't let the matter end there. As coloured communities we need to take pride in our self-worth as a people but also be brutally honest and own the many shortcomings that we can positively change.

However, it would be an incorrect strategy to make this a coloured battle alone. What I think should happen is that coloured communities should form an alliance with predominantly African communities such as Langa, Nyanga, Khayelitsha, and Lwandle to tackle these problems and also hold the government to account. They should not let political parties hijack these grassroots initiatives and momentum.

Furthermore, many educated coloured graduates or entrepreneurs move out of the coloured communities because they want to provide their children with better educational opportunities and safer environments in which to live. The drawback is that skills, competencies and leadership capacity moves out of these communities and therefore little is done by these graduates and entrepreneurs in paying forward for the next generation.

The challenge is that all graduates and entrepreneurs should invest at least 30 hours a year in focused grassroots opportunities to uplift the youth through skills workshops, social entrepreneurial projects, and mentorship. They should be visible as role models that youth can aspire to instead of aspiring to be gangsters with money and flashy cars.

I am advocating the broadening of young people's definition of success and what can be achieved. Success could be defined as being a social entrepreneur conducting projects that impact community wellbeing or following a vocation that involves being closer to God. We should remove the idea that the only measure to gauge success is money. However, each person is entitled to a minimum level of attainment with regards to socio-economic rights.

Lastly, adversity such as socio-economic challenges do not need to be a stumbling block but could be a catalyst for success. Winston Churchhill said:

> *The stern compression of circumstances, the twinges of adversity, the spur of slights and taunts in early years, are needed to evoke that ruthless fixity of purpose and tenacious motherwit without which great actions are seldom accomplished.*[43]

Questions

1. Do you, as coloured parents, know and understand your personal lineage and family history tree?
2. Do your children know and understand your personal lineage and family history tree?
3. Are we providing alternative role models to criminals in our townships?
4. What are you doing in terms of paying forward for the next generation?

Steps that can be taken

1. Learn about your history, culture and identity.
2. Encourage history to be taught in a holistic way take into account the contribution, experience, culture, identity and struggles of all racial groups.

11. THE ROLE OF SCHOOLS

Our children are the rock on which our future will be built;
our greatest asset as a nation. They will be the leaders of
our country, the creators of our national wealth who care
for and protect our people.

—*Nelson Mandela*

In 1999 the Human Rights Commission Report titled "Racism, racial integration and desegregation in South Africa public secondary schools"[44] stated that they had investigated many complaints dealing with discrimination in disciplinary measures, racial violence, and cultural prejudice. The Commission indicated that the character of schools was based on racial separation and discrimination. Endeavours to effect racial integration have not borne the fruits envisaged. Learners whose parents have taught them ingrained prejudices bring those opinions and views to school. Schools have inadequate anti-racism mechanisms to prepare learners to value human dignity, equality, diversity, non-racialism.

The Commission found that educators have shown very little or no commitment to creating a learning environment free from discrimination and prejudice. Many educators gave in to their own biases and preferred to deny the existence of racism, or their conduct conformed to superficial tolerance. When some educators did attempt cultural assimilation, it took the form of tolerating black learners instead of affirming that these black children had a right to be there. Since the start of the democratic era, there have been numerous clashes between white and black learners and parents demanding significant transformation at schools, especially at formerly white schools. Education has become less important than the ongoing struggle for change.

To a large extent, the above is still true in many Model C schools. These schools are the coalface where children of all races converge, though the overwhelming majority of the children are white and from privileged backgrounds.

Although almost twenty years have elapsed from the date this report was issued, South African schools still grapple with the same problems. Model C schools struggle with racial integration and with developing and implementing the policies and procedures that enforce anti-racism behaviour. In recent years, the national media has shown how racism has damaged various schools' reputations. Racism is not good business. Governing bodies, principals and parents of children in Model C schools are not doing enough to ensure racism is uprooted and discarded.

Many black people perceive that racism exists and thrives in the Model C school environment because of the conduct of specific school governing bodies (SGBs), principals, parents, classmates, and educators.

Further, in my opinion, the school's leadership, including the headmaster/headmistress and SGB, lack the capacity to adequately lead racial integration programmes. They are overwhelmed or defensive when racial tension occurs during the process. Furthermore, the leadership requires the vision and competencies to forge a diverse new school culture and not choose the easier route of assimilating the new black learners in the current culture.

Sometimes leaders become creative in limiting the intake of non-white students to Model C schools. One way is when an Afrikaans dominated school limits the number of English speaking classes. Most Africans are not proficient in Afrikaans, and therefore they will struggle to obtain placement as limited places exist for English speaking children. Professor Jonathan Jansen, a well know education specialist, states that when the non-white student component in a Model C school moves above 50 per cent you will find a white flight from that particular school.[45] Why?

Further, the SGBs will limit the number of non-white educators appointed at the school. White teachers are equated with quality education so the SGB will restrict the affirmative action policies and the number of black appointments. However, the African and coloured elite also perpetuates this false and racist notion by insisting that their children also attend a majority white managed school with a majority white population.

Another area associated with subtle racism relates to the school's communication practice. In a multiracial school, especially in a dual language school, educators inadequately accommodate English speaking parents where the parent base is predominately Afrikaans. Communication practice is especially prevalent in sports meetings. What happens is that white educators address the pleasantries in English and substantive matters in Afrikaans. However, I have been at meetings where African parents attend with limited Afrikaans understanding. The conversation goes something like this:

> *Good evening parents. Die kinders speel Saterdag in Durbanville. Hulle moet 9:30 daar wees. Ons sal 8:30 hier ontmoet 08:30 en die kinders met die bus deurvat. Hulle moet die volgende toerusting saamvat. Thank you, parents, for coming. Have a safe trip home.*

This example demonstrates that no attempt is made to communicate the substantive arrangement to non-Afrikaans speaking parents, especially African parents.

Why?

The conduct by some educators is not conducive to creating an environment that is perceived as accommodating to nonracialism. Although limited positive strides to address learner racial diversity has been made in the private school and Model C school environments, normal public-school environments like the one I attended in Bonteheuwel remain unintegrated, under-resourced and plagued by various social ills of the community. Furthermore, the principle of demand and supply results in the Model C schools having the funds to attract the more educated and skilled educators to these schools. A lot has still to be done to the demographic profile of students and teachers reflect the diversity in South Africa. Failure to achieve this remains a considerable obstacle to ensure faster integration and social cohesion.

One of the most contentious areas in a school environment that gets parents (especially black parents) despondent and angry is the issue of sports team selection. Here the selection process is arbitrary at best. Selection criteria are fluid. No attempt is made to maintain or develop an objective selection process. School sports administrators and coaches seem to have limited emotional intelligence as to the impact their decisions have on the dignity and psyches of the children in their care. Most, if not all, coaches are white in Model C schools and black parents perceive the selection process to be biased and some coaches to be racists.

Many of these challenges could be avoided or mitigated by having a coherent approach to foster anti-racism and value diversity. It is imperative that the school have an anti-racism policy. This policy should, as a minimum, address the following:

1. the meaning of racism
2. what will constitute a racist incident
3. what is expected from the child
4. what is expected from educators and SGB
5. where a child should go to report an alleged racial incident
6. what action should be taken by the school.

Schools should have meaningful programmes to address racism and foster diversity and should not only pay lip service. If we want schools to indeed promote nonracialism, schools must fully commit to an anti-racism agenda and measures. Educators and SGBs must be adequately trained regarding what is expected of them. Training and review of actions must be continuous to ensure we are achieving the desired results.

However, if schools and SGBs continue to resist transformation, parents could collectively decide to use creative strategies to litigate for the protection of human dignity and the eradication of racism. This may result in a faster and more significant change; however, it might not achieve the desired objective of social cohesion.

Collectively, educators and parents must pay particular attention to the development and formation of a child's conscience. This development of a child's conscience is impacted by the stories, narratives, societal views, customs and traditions they come into contact with. These elements shape a child's character and world view and will impact the decisions they make in the future.[46]

Questions

1. Is the school leadership communicated to non-racialism?
2. Do you have the correct leader for the job?
3. Does your school have an anti-racism policy?
4. Do you have a comprehensive communication strategy to accommodate your diverse group of parents?
5. Have the educators been trained on the anti-racism policy and measures?
6. Does the school have objective criteria for the selection of school sports teams?
7. Does the school communicate these criteria to learners and parents?
8. Has the school done a child impact assessment about decisions in respect to racism at school?

Steps to be taken

1. Have the right leadership that will respect, promote, and ensure the human dignity of each learner is protected.
2. Have a vision and strategy that moves towards having a school that reflects the demographic profile of South Africa.
3. Have an anti-racism policy and programme.
4. Improve the demographic profile of educators.
5. Train educators regarding values and conduct that is expected of them in respect of non-racialism.
6. SGBs must ensure that performance contracts with educators have performance objectives related to the implementation of anti-racism measures.
7. Have key performance measures that school management must attain in terms of implementation of anti-racism measures.
8. Have a succession and skills development plan in place to ensure a more equitable demographic profile for educators. Meritocracy and the attainment of anti-racism measures need not be mutually exclusive.

9. Consider the use of creative strategies to litigate, bearing in mind that this might have unintended consequences.

12. THE ROLE OF HIGHER EDUCATION

From a young age, I knew that to escape the chronic, severe and challenging financial circumstances we experienced in Bonteheuwel I had to educate myself to create better career prospects. I knew that I had to work hard academically, but I also had to try and assist my parents by finding casual employment to gain extra income.

During my high school days, I earned money for my travelling costs from home to school by working as general labourer at a local newspaper distribution depot or at the factory where my father was employed.

When I studied full time for three years, I generated funds by working as a security officer in a clothing store on Saturdays and some school holidays. However, the bulk of my studies was completed over many years via distance learning while having a full-time job and family to feed. The only course paid by my employer was the non-academic Nexus programme at GIBS mentioned earlier in the text.

Therefore, it is difficult for me, having these lived experiences, to understand why some students do not make a bigger and focused effort to generate funds for their studies. This might not be the politically correct view.

Today in South Africa, higher education is very volatile because of protests by students in favour of free higher education (pro-poor) and decolonisation. I support this initiative 90% (not 100%) as I do believe that higher education should not be the preserve of the rich but should be available to all academically deserving students.

My reason for not supporting the students 100% is because I believe that at times student do not appreciate the inequality they create when forcefully advocating for their rights in direct opposition to sectors of our communities that cannot energetically promote for their equitable share of government budgets. As an example, spending more on tertiary education will reduce the amount available for childcare and earlier phases of education, thus robbing children of the right to primary education, shelter and health. It is unfortunate that vulnerable children cannot use pressure tactics to assert their rights.

I do understand that I was fortunate to obtain casual work, as systemic issues in our economy do not allow everyone to gain casual employment. However, I do believe that students could do more to assist in covering their fees. The government just does not have enough money to provide for higher education for all students. But do not let this stop you; you must move forward one step at a time even if this means one module at a time through distance learning with UNISA.

The South African Constitution requires the State to take reasonable legislative and other measures, within its available resources, to achieve the progressive realisation of socio-economic rights like education and health. I do not believe the State has done enough to promote the attainment of socio-economic rights. This is as a result of state capture, corruption, sometimes incompetence, etc. What we should be advocating is the introduction of a minimum level of socio-economic rights. The minimum core obligations will apply regardless of the availability of resources of South Africa or any other challenges. This will force the South African State to look for creative strategies to provide for the minimum core entitlements for all socio-economic rights. But it will equally put pressure on recipients such as students to work to achieve the difference between the minimum core and actual fee required to attain the qualification.

Historical legacies of colonialism and apartheid, including current academics' behaviour of spreading racist views and racial propaganda, is negatively affecting race relations in higher education. There seems to be a lack of collegiality and respect between black and white scholars. Some white academics' conduct is problematic as it is based on racial stereotype, discrimination and blatant racism. There seems to at times be the perception that black academics cannot be experts on the specific subject matter and cannot produce knowledge.

An excellent example of the lack of collegiality and respect amongst black and white academics is the racist incidents at South Africa's leading distance university, UNISA. There were allegations of discrimination, racism, sexism and harassment at the institution. The South African Human Rights Commission (SAHRC) held public hearings to test the veracity of allegations that senior academics were racists and white supremacists. Further, claims were made that individual professors were preventing transformation at the law faculty. A general breakdown in the professional relationships between white and black academics arose. Some white academics felt physically threatened and feared going to their offices.

The SAHRC made a broad set of recommendations to implement change at the university. My concern with the developments at this particular university is that the relationship breakdown occurred between educated people. These people should have developed the emotional intelligence and conflict resolution skills to address these underlying perceptions and sometimes blatant comments that impaired the dignity of others. There is such a lot of resentment and unresolved anger regarding racism that reason can sometimes not prevail.

As I am completing this book, two other racism scandals are erupting at two prominent South African universities. One is at UCT where another independent panel is alleging racism at UCT. Another set of recommendations will most probably flow from the esteemed panel. My hopes and prayers are that meaningful anti-racism and decolonisation measures are implemented to really change the psyche of white academics and the institutional culture at some prominent universities.

The second scandal has really made many people angry, especially coloured women. It is a "study" undertaken by white researchers that allege that coloured South African women have lower cognitive abilities due to their lifestyle and poor education. Some professors have robustly criticised the "research paper"[47] based on scientific and academic grounds. Some academics have viewed the study as quite racist.

More importantly, the critics have raised concerns with the whole colonial peer review process for evaluating the research article. The research proposal was cleared by the Ethical Clearance Committee, it received funding, it was submitted to an academic journal and reviewed by an editor and after that by at least two other reviewers in the specific academic field. None of these internal controls highlighted a potential risk for flawed results. Did all the people involve harbour the same racist beliefs?

Leaders at these universities must realise that they have an enormous social responsibility to address these underlying resentment from blacks and whites and they should implement sustainable programmes that entrench the constitutional values within the organisations.

Questions

1. Has racism become so ingrained in the centres of higher learning that leadership and white students and academics do not see it?

Steps to be taken

1. Action the various reports produced over the last 20 years that dealt with racism.

13. THE ROLE OF THE CHURCH

The Church cannot and must not take upon herself the political battle to bring about a most just society possible. She cannot and must not replace the State. Yet at the same time she cannot and must not remain on the sidelines in the fight for justice. She has to play her part through national argument, and she has to reawaken the spiritual energy without which justice, which always demands sacrifice, cannot prevail and proposer. A just society must be the achievement of politics, not of Christ. Yet the promotion of justice through efforts to bring about openness of mind and will to the demands of the common good is something which concerns the Church deeply.

—*Deus Caritas, EST, No 28*

I am a Catholic. I have been raised in a home where my parents were passionate about the things of God. As children, we were taught that God should be the centre of our lives. We attended regular prayer meetings. Our home was a typical small two-bedroom house in Bonteheuwel. However, it was unique in that when you entered our family home, you immediately noticed an altar. The altar was built to reflect the architecture of Schoenstatt in Constantia. On this altar, my mom always had a candle burning if she was praying for a particular intention. This could include her sons travelling by train late the evening, or one of her children writing examinations or one of the family sick.

At Christmas, we decorated the altar and Dad had various ornaments and statues depicting Christ Jesus' birth in the stable. During Lent and Easter, Dad would decorate the altar to reflect the period that Catholics and Christians, in general, were celebrating.

In the same lounge where the altar was situated were portraits of the stations of the cross. My dad and mom always used to seal us with the sign of the cross on our foreheads when we left the house or when Dad went off to work.

Further, during a difficult time in our lives, the Church supported us as a family. We used to belong to the Schoenstatt family group. During the period when my father was not working, the Schoenstatt nuns use to travel from Constantia regularly to bring us food. I know as a young boy eating this white cheese, they brought that had a funny taste. The nuns also use to bring skim milk for us to drink. The church not only fed us spiritually but physically with the assistance the nuns gave.

I am stating the above because I do have a bias to Catholicism as this was the vehicle that helped me find a relationship with my saviour Christ Jesus. Further, through difficult times in my formative years and the formative years of my siblings, we felt and experienced the nurture and support of the Catholic Church.

I really believe that Catholicism has an enormous role to play in addressing some of the social ills of the world. Today, everyone knows about the issues of child abuse within the Catholic Church that have damaged its reputation. Similarly, the inadequate assistance in proactively addressing racism has and will continue to create disunity with the church.

My perspective and opinion mainly relate to the Catholic Church which I am a member of. However, the concerns, risks, challenges and recommendations could be applied to other denominations.

The evil of prejudice and racism has been with us as Christians for more than 2,000 years. In Galatians 3 verse 26–28 it reads "for in Christ Jesus you are all sons of God, through faith. For as many of you as were baptized into Christ have put on Christ. There is neither Jew nor Greek, there is neither slave or free, there is neither male nor female; for you are all one in Christ Jesus."[48]

The Apostle Paul is responding to the Jewish Christians and articulates the value of equality. Although Christ Jesus was a Jew, it was not a requirement for a Christian to be a Jew. He explained forcefully that there should be no prejudice against the Greeks

(Gentiles). This text makes it clear that no advantage is given to a particular race or people.

Just as in early Christian days, the world continues to struggle with prejudice and racism. Especially in the United States of America. As far back as 1979, the United States Conference of Bishops issued a pastoral letter on racism called *Brothers and Sisters to Us*. In 2003, Bishop Melczek of the Diocese of Gary wrote a pastoral letter called *Created in God's image: Proposal Letter on the Sin of racism and a Call to Conversion.* He advocates that racism should be addressed using an interdisciplinary approach and that psychology and sociology could assist in better understanding racism.[49] For Melczek, racism manifests itself in society on an individual, cultural, and institutional level.

Further, the Bishop proposes several responses to racism:
1. to methodically examine racism
2. as parents, to address the sin of racism with their children
3. to persuade Christians to have a more inclusive vision, and
4. to strive in solidarity towards racial justice.

Similarly, Archbishop Harry Flynn of the Diocese of Saint Paul and Minneapolis, reminds Catholics in his pastoral letter called *God's Image: Pastoral Letter on Racism* that the gospel commands the Church take decisive steps to address the personal and social manifestations of racism.[50]

Again in 2018, the United States Catholic Bishops Conference issued a pastoral letter condemning racism.[51] The letter states that when an individual's racist views cause him or her to exclude, mistreat or unjustly discriminate against any person, then it is sinful.

The Vatican's Pontifical Council for Justice and Peace published a document on racism, titled *Church and Racism: Towards a more fraternal society.* The document outlines the Catholic Church's position and its teaching against racism. The core of this document emphasises the belief that every person is created in God's image and every person is provided redemption through the paschal mystery.

The Pontifical Council for Justice and Peace articulates racism as a form of blasphemy and recommends tackling it through educational and structural changes in every level of society.[52] The aim is to advocate for equality for all minority groups and to respect and promote each other's cultural and religious characteristics. The document further emphasises that racism exists in every society.

The approaches outlined above is sound. However, the eradication of racism is elusive because since 1979 little has changed in the US race relations and, as an outsider, I would say it has deteriorated.

It seems that the Catholic family takes a fragmented approach to dealing with global issues such as racism. Even worse, one region does not learn from the mistakes, research or successful approaches taken in different geographical areas. This has also been highlighted with regards to child sexual abuse.

There have been some robust approaches and proper investigations and recommendations made in addressing child sexual abuse that could be used to tackle racism. The Catholic Church has approximately 1 billion members and has enormous influence in the world. Does the Church lack the institutional will to really combat racism in all the territories where it is positioned?

The McLellan Commission, which investigated child abuse, stated the following in respect for child abuse.

> *There is no place in safeguarding for paying "lip service" to the necessity of good training: the risks are too high. There is no place for creating training schemes without making absolutely sure that everyone participates in them. There is no place for the view that once in a lifetime is enough training. Training must be both general and specific. Everyone must know the law . . . . In addition, each person must know the particular responsibilities belonging to his or her role. Training produces good practice and develops confidence.[53]*

This is true in the context of safeguarding of children but equally true about racism. There is no room to pay lip service to this massive global societal challenge, but particularly in South Africa. The risks are just too high. Churches are institutions that yield persuasive power are well suited to be the catalyst for addressing racism. Also, the skillset and tools required to engage with the topic of racism already exist within the Church. In the Catholic Church in Cape Town, they have a restorative justice programme that reconciles victims of crime with perpetrators. However, the Church could adapt the restorative programme to kickstart the racism engagement process. The Church could provide a loving, supportive, safe platform and means to start the meaningful engagement between different racial groups.

Churches in South Africa could learn from the United Church of Canada's Anti-Racism Policy Statement.[54] Here is its statement of beliefs:

> *We believe we are all equal before God.*
>
> *We believe racism is a sin and violates God's desire for humanity.*
>
> *We believe racism is present in our society and in our church, and throughout time has manifested itself in many forms to varying degrees.*
>
> *We believe that the struggle against racism is a continuous effort. Therefore, our anti-racism policy statement is only a first step. It provides the basis for the creation of a church where all are welcome, where all feel welcome, and where diversity is as natural as breathing.*
>
> *We believe change is possible. We believe in forgiveness, reconciliation, and transformation and the potential to learn from stories and experiences.*
>
> *We believe we are called to work against racism and for a society in which the words of the gospel are realized among us.*
>
> *We believe in a vision of society in which these words of the gospel are realized.*

Wow! What a powerful statement to make. The above statement, in addition to other resources that the United Church of Canada has developed, is a substantive effort to address racism. The United Church of Canada has provided a model statement that all churches in South Africa should adopt.

Questions

1. In what way has your church neglected to confront racism?
2. Are there ways in which your faith sharing group/community can help different races to feel more included?
3. Are you learning from other members' stories and experiences?

Steps that the church and faith communities could take

1. Action the recommendations contained in various reports.
2. Learn from other geographical regions struggling with racism.
3. Create platforms to share prejudice and racism stories and experiences.
4. Use the internal skills and competencies in terms of restorative justice to facilitate meaningful dialogue.

14. THE ROLE OF CORPORATE SOUTH AFRICA

During the apartheid era, the corporate sector refused to acknowledge the exploitation, undermining and oppression of black people in South Africa. Today in some circles within corporate South Africa, the undermining of black people persists.

In July 2018 a coloured sports presenter by the name of Ashwell Willemse, a World Cup winning member of the Springbok rugby team, disagreed with two of his fellow rugby commentators on live television. His two colleagues were white and had played rugby for South Africa in the apartheid era.

Ashwell stated that these two rugby commentators undermined his contribution as a Springbok rugby player and referred to him as a quota player.[55] A quota player is perceived to be a member of the team selected to ensure some non-white representation in the group.[56] A quota player is seen to not be chosen on merit. Many of the non-white rugby players who have been selected on merit are still not seen as being part of the team on merit.

There is a general perception amongst some white people that any non-white appointment in business, government or sports departments are the result of affirmative action and not merit-based. This perception could not be further from the truth. Many black appointments do have the requisite education, experience and ability to occupy these positions.

I take myself as an example. I studied continuously for about 22 years. Three years full time and the rest by distance learning while receiving the appropriate experiential training and exposure. I attained the National Diploma in Cost and Management Accounting and qualified as a Professional Accountant (SA) and Chartered Management Accountant. Also, I completed a Master of Business Administration degree, Bachelor of Laws degree and

Master of Laws degree. I have recently passed my Doctorate in Laws degree.

Further, I am an admitted Advocate of the High Court of South Africa. I worked in the corporate world managing billions in procurement spend and supervising different staff in multiple geographical locations. I was not a quota or affirmative action candidate. My skin colour maybe gave me a slight advantage with affirmative action policies, however, I had to work extremely hard to get educated and gain the necessary experience. I am not unique! There are many qualified black people that have conquered many obstacles and challenges to qualify for the positions they occupy. They deserve their rewards.

Further, I have left the comfort of the corporate world, initially taking a significant salary knock and risking my capital to become an entrepreneur. I feel with a person like Ashwell when white men refer to him as a token/quota player. Like myself, he has worked his butt off and has excelled in his chosen profession. That racist bias that we merely rocked up and got the job is nonsense.

Sometimes I think employment equity policies are a convenient excuse for some white men. They would never excel in sport or business but use employment equity as an excuse for not being successful or not obtaining promotion or rewards.

However, I have managed many young white men who reported to me while working in the corporate world. My subordinates had a different academic background, including having engineering degrees, while others had more business-related degrees. Many of them were very talented, hardworking and loyal. But they could not progress further up the corporate ladder. I had to mentor and encourage them to still give their best, and they did!

It is essential for leaders to connect as I did on a personal level with colleagues and subordinates, respecting and acknowledging the gifts and talents. Together, try to find ways for all teammates to grow, even if that does not mean promotion. I am still in contact with a few of these young and older men that I have learnt from, and hopefully, in turn, they gained something from their interaction with me. But more importantly, it was a personal commitment that has been sustained throughout these years.

I have also had leaders in corporates that have mentored and supported me in my career and personal development. Most of them, because of apartheid legacies, were white. But most were decent, God-fearing and competent leaders that, like me, we also grappling with their tasks and roles in the corporate space.

On a more strategic level, we need to see the transformation happening that will result in a more equitable distribution of income. Unfortunately, because the owners of capital are white, there must be an equitable distribution of income from white to black unless we can increase the size of the economy. I am not the biggest fan of black empowerment as only a particular portion of the black elite benefits. What I think should happen is that the equitable distribution of income must lead to the realisation and attainment of socio-economic rights for all South Africa citizens. Until this happens, very little will change in terms of the face of poverty in South Africa. It will remain overwhelmingly black.

Questions

1. Are you meaningfully engaging as a leader with your subordinates on a personal level about transformation and explaining the necessity for it correctly?
2. Are you having a frank and honest conversation regarding career opportunities and about creative ways to live out their latent potential?
3. Are you using affirmative action policies as a crutch for your lack of achievement?
4. Are you using apartheid as a crutch for your lack of achievement?

Steps that can be taken

1. Support transformation projects.
2. Share your stories, experiences, goals and concerns with your colleagues and leaders in a constructive manner.
3. Corporate leaders and politicians should consider a different economic transformation model in South Africa that is much more focused on changing the socio-economic conditions of all South Africans, not only the black elite.

15. THE ROLE OF THE HUMAN RIGHTS COMMISSION AND EQUALITY COURTS

One of the leading institutions that has a role to play in the eradication of racism is the South African Human Rights Commission (SAHRC), a Chapter 9 institution. The SAHRC's roles, power and authority are outlined in the Human Rights Commission Act (HRCA) (54 of 1994). The SAHRC is responsible for:
1. increasing the awareness of human rights issues
2. monitoring and assessing human rights observance
3. educating and training society on human rights
4. addressing human rights violations and seeking effective redress.

Also, the HRCA empowers the SAHRC to investigate and subpoena individuals, to enter and search premises, and to remove relevant evidence from such premises.[57] The SAHRC is authorised to investigate complaints of alleged human rights violations.[58] If the SAHRC finds the claim has merit after investigating the matter, it can assist the complainant in obtaining redress. However, if the parties do not comply with the SAHRC recommendations, the courts must be approached to help with enforcement.

I view the SAHRC as firefighters. Every time a problem flares up, they are there to douse the flames. As good firefighters they provide us with specific tips and reports that we must implement to prevent fires. However, what we require are sustainable and systematic programmes to ensure the eradication of racism and the protection of human rights. If not we will still be having the same conversations regarding racism 20 years from now.

The Constitution and the HRCA require different branches of government to cooperate fully with the SAHRC in its efforts to discharge its mandate. Practically this means that the government must make sufficient funds available for the SAHRC to implement sustainable programmes. The cost of these programmes could be significant; however, if we are going to change the psyche and fabric of all South Africans it will require considerable investment in resources so that the SAHRC can fully discharge its mandate.

Since its inception, the SAHRC has mainly focused on two areas in the last decade, namely the combating of racism and the promotion of socio-economic rights.[59] Although the SAHRC has regularly published Economic and Social Rights Reports, it has not lived up to its mandate to advance socio-economic rights.[60] To the general public, the role and the work of the SAHRC are not known because it has not advocated the interest of the marginalised sufficiently. Critics believe that the SAHRC could play a more significant role, in line with its constitutional and statutory mandate, in improving judicial enforcement of economic and social rights.

The SAHRC is an important body that should protect and promote human rights in South Africa. However, I believe that it has not done enough to educate and assist with the transformation of our society to reflect our core values of human dignity, equality and freedom. More could be done to really embed a human rights culture within our communities and to indeed ensure that our children become ambassadors of human rights and have an inbuilt anti-racism belief system.

Questions

1. Do you understand the work the SAHRC is doing?
2. Are you proactively supporting the work of the SAHRC in your church, children's schools, etc.?
3. Do you understand the work of the Equality Court?
4. Do you understand what constitutes hate speech?
5. Do you understand all the consequences of transgression the Promotion of Equality and Prevention of Unfair Discrimination Act (The Equality Act)?

Steps to be taken

1. Roll out programmes that will ensure children become ambassadors of human rights and have an anti-racism belief system.
2. Put pressure on the SAHRC to educate and train society on human rights, to address human rights violations and to seek effective redress.

16. THE ROLE OF THE STATE

International treaties oblige State parties to respect, protect and promote human rights. One of the most fundamental human rights that racism negatively impacts is the right to human dignity. Human dignity is an inalienable right. The concept of dignity is central to all other rights and is also contained in the preamble of the United Nations Declaration of Human Rights, which recognises that the inherent dignity and equal rights "of all members of the human family is the foundation of freedom, justice and peace in the world".[61]

In conformity with international law, the South African Constitution has human dignity as one of its foundational values. Therefore the State has several legal duties, as described below:

Respect

The State must protect the enjoyment of human rights and refrain from interfering with the exercise of human rights.[62]

Protect

The obligation to protect places a duty on the State to prohibit third parties from interfering with the enjoyment of human rights.[63] Thus, the State must adopt legislation and other measures that prevent any party from interfering with the rights of beneficiaries. The duty to protect is a positive duty.

Promote

The obligation to promote requires the State to disseminate relevant and appropriate information, to encourage research and support people to make informed choices.[64]

Ensure

The obligation to ensure obliges the State to implement the required measures that advance the achievement of the full realisation of human rights.[65] The objective of this obligation is to ensure that people who do not currently have access to this right, gain access. The requirement to ensure obliges the State to facilitate and implement legislative and other measures in recognition of the right.

Furthermore, the State is obliged to adopt national policies with detailed plans on how to realise the right.

The South African State has a legal duty to respect, protect, promote and ensure the human dignity of every person. Part of this duty is to facilitate and implement legislative and other measures to counteract racism. In my humble opinion, we will not do justice to this foundational value of human dignity if we do not at the same time facilitate and implement legislative and other measures to fully attain the socio-economic rights of all people living in South Africa.

Because of the legacy of colonialism, apartheid, and the current corruption and unethical leadership, millions of our compatriots still live in abject poverty. Aggravating this is forced unemployment due to systemic problems in our economy that cannot create enough jobs for all South Africans, leading to the non-realisation of their socio-economic rights (education, health, shelter, nutrition). Further, because socio-economic rights are subject to progressive realisation depending on government resources (budgets), the government can use this as a convenient excuse.

Although the middle class (which is overwhelming white because of past racial, historical structures) may be upset, the courts, the executive government and the public, in general, must ensure that a minimum level of socio-economic rights that accords with the human dignity of persons is maintained. Just as the property clause is sacrosanct for landowners, the realisation of socio-economic rights for the poor is sacrosanct. We need to be passionate about all constitutional rights and should not cherry pick.

Let me make the minimum level argument clearer by referring to two Constitutional Court (CC) Cases. *The Government of SA v*

Grootboom and others[66] and *Soobramoney v Minister of Health, KwaZulu-Natal.*[67] The Grootboom case dealt with the right to have access to adequate housing of several homeless people who were expelled from shelters built on private land. Mrs Irene Grootboom and the other respondents were rendered homeless after being evicted from their informal homes situated on private land earmarked for formal low-cost housing.

Mrs Grootboom and the other respondents applied to the Cape of Good Hope High Court for an order requiring the government to provide them with adequate basic shelter or housing until they obtained permanent accommodation and were granted specific relief. The appellants were ordered to provide the respondents who were children and their parents with shelter. The judgment provisionally concluded, "tents, portable latrines and a regular supply of water (albeit transported) would constitute the bare minimum". The appellants, who represented all spheres of government responsible for housing, challenged the correctness of that order.

In the CC the *amici curiae* submitted that a minimum core obligation exists with regards to the right of access to adequate housing in terms of s 26(1) of the Constitution. The *amici curiae* argued that the Court should enforce this minimum entitlement. The CC declined to do so, saying:

> *It is not possible to determine the minimum threshold for the progressive realisation of the right of access to adequate housing without first identifying the needs and opportunities for the enjoyment of such a right. These will vary according to factors such as income, availability of land and poverty... Variations ultimately depend on the economic and social history of a country. All this illustrates the complexity of the task of determining a minimum core obligation for the progressive realisation of the right of access to adequate housing without having the requisite information on the needs and the opportunities for the enjoyment of this right.*[68]

The CC stated that rather than define and enforce a minimum core obligation inherent in s 26, the CC has to decide whether the current State policy about housing delivery was reasonable under s 26(2). Applying the reasonableness standard, the CC found that the challenged housing policy was unreasonable, principally because it did not make reasonable provision for the emergency needs of vulnerable groups. The chosen governmental actions should be reasonable both in their conception and in their implementation.[69] The CC stated that the Constitution provided that the right to housing was dependent upon available resources.

The CC acknowledged that the ICESCR, an international treaty, imposes minimum core obligation on the State but that the ICESCR in its General Comment "does not specify precisely what the minimum core is" with regards to socio-economic rights.[70] The CC's view was that ICESCR was able to develop the minimum core concept based on extensive experience gained from examining reports on State compliance with the ICESCR's obligations over many years.

Furthermore, the CC stated that an evaluation must be made as to whether the measures taken by the State to realise the right afforded by s 26 were reasonable. The CC expressed concern that in the absence of comparable information and evidence, it was challenging to define the minimum core in the domestic context.

Nevertheless, commentators and others continue to debate as to how the CC's approach could be strengthened given potential limits on judicial competence and legitimacy.[71] Debate continues on whether the CC could legitimately have opted for a more expansive and more defined interpretation with regards to the nature of individual socio-economic rights under the South African Constitution.

In *Soobramoney v Minister of Health, KwaZulu-Natal*[72] the CC was called upon to adjudicate on the ambit of socio-economic rights. The appellant was a 41-year-old unemployed man and a diabetic. Also, the appellant suffered from ischaemic heart disease and cerebrovascular disease that caused him to have a stroke in 1996. In 1996 his kidneys also failed.

His condition was irreversible, and Mr Soobramoney was in the final stages of chronic renal failure. His life could have been prolonged using regular renal dialysis. Only a limited number of patients were given this treatment at Addington Hospital. The renal unit had 20 dialysis machines available, some of which were in poor condition. Each treatment was four hours long, whereafter a further two hours was necessary to clean the device before another use. The limitation on the availability of the renal dialysis machines made it impossible for Addington Hospital to administer renal dialysis treatment to Mr Soobramoney.

The High Court's analysis of this case commenced by evaluating the negative nature of the right enshrined in s 27(3), and that it does not create a right to emergency medical treatment.[73] In the Court's view, s 27(3) created a negative right "not to be refused emergency medical treatment". This means that the treatment must already be "possible and available" and the right is not to have that available emergency treatment refused. This view meant that the right is contextually constrained by the existing resources, which is ultimately subjected to budgetary constraints.

The applicants argued that budgetary constraints that the State might experience are not a legitimate reason to refuse adequate medical treatment since this right is constitutionally entrenched. The Court accepted the applicant's contention. However, the Court nonetheless went on to say that budgetary considerations were still relevant in determining what constitutes "adequate medical treatment". Based on these facts, the Court held that the State had not proved that they could not afford anti-retroviral treatment for prisoners. Consequently, the Court ordered that the State provide ARVs to applicants.

Mr Soobramoney approached the Courts and based his claim on s 27(3) of the 1996 Constitution that states, "No one may be refused emergency medical treatment" and s 11 that stipulates "Everyone has the right to life".[74] The Court refused the application for relief.

Soobramoney appealed to the CC, relying on s 11 (the right to life) and again on s 27(3). Chaskalson P, for the majority judgment, found that the right to life could not be used to ground a claim for emergency medical treatment since such a right was already explicitly provided for in s 27(3). Nonetheless, the Court rejected the argument that the treatment claimed constituted "emergency medical treatment". The CC judgment closed the door on an opportunity to interpret the right to life more broadly as being inclusive of socio-economic rights that are contained elsewhere in the Constitution. Therefore, the CC's interpretation has restricted all claims of socio-economic rights under the qualified rights in ss 26 and 27.

The CC stated that Mr Soobramoney's demand to receive dialysis treatment at a State hospital must be determined by the provisions of ss 27(1) and (2) and not s 27(3). The CC stated further that these provisions entitle everyone to have access to health care services provided by the State "within its available resources". Trispiotis argued that the CC erred by dismissing the claim of a chronically ill and non-curable patient, whose denial of dialysis treatment amounted to a breach of his right to emergency medical treatment. Further, he argues that a wide margin of discretion accorded to the provincial government as far as budget priorities were concerned, was incorrect.

Although our Constitutional Court has been applauded for its progressive judgments, generally, it has not been bold enough in protecting and promoting the full realisation of socio-economic rights. Further, I believe they made a mistake to use a utilitarian approach, i.e. what is best for the common good of all instead of an examination of the impact the decision has on the dignity of each person.

I think that maybe Professor Terblanche's argument regarding a wealth tax as explained earlier is not a bad idea considering we could ring-fence those funds specifically to improve the socio-economic conditions of the poor.

This imbalance between the affluent (mostly white) and poor (mostly black) is not sustainable. This imbalance is systematic racism as it has a disproportionally adverse effect on blacks. We need to ensure that all citizens' human dignity is protected by ensuring the full realisation of socio-economic rights. If not, the lived experience of blacks will lead them to resent white people mainly, but the middle class in particular, and might lead to a violent confrontation to realise socio-economic rights.

The province of Ontario in Canada has a systematic approach to tackle racism. They have a three-year strategic plan in which they commit to change the way they do things and break down barriers that hinder racial equity.[75]

The South African government, on the other hand, has a shotgun and knee-jerk approach to tackling racism. A three-year strategic plan with well-documented metrics and a robust monitoring and evaluation mechanism will go a long way in combating racism. There have been reports in the media that the South African government is busy compiling such a plan. But so far we have nothing to show for it.

Questions

1. Are you an advocate for the full realisation of socio-economic rights?
2. If not, why not?
3. Should we not have a national dialogue regarding racism, combatting racism and social cohesion?
4. What would a proactive government strategy to eradicate racism and promote social cohesion look like?
5. How can we, individually and collectively, put pressure on the government to develop such strategy and actions?

Steps that can be taken

1. Have a national dialogue on racism, combatting racism and social cohesion.
2. Have a three-year strategic plan to combat racism
3. Have mandatory training for educators and learners.

SUMMARY

That which you persist in doing becomes easier to do, not that the task itself has become easier, but that our ability to perform it has improved.

—*Ralph Waldo Emerson, American poet and essayist*

Social transformation, including anti-racism measures, will take many years to bear fruit. However, to achieve social cohesion, we as a nation must collectively put our shoulders to the wheel. We must embrace, respect and promote our diversity and develop the skill to meaningfully dialogue. It is only through meaningful dialogue that we will understand different perspectives.

Throughout this book, I have shared my stories about racism and race relations in South Africa. We are a nation of enormous wealth and human potential. I remain optimistic about our nation future and that all children whether African, coloured, white or Indian will reach their full potential provided we create the enabling environment for frank and open dialogue about contentious subjects such as history, land, wealth distribution and meritocracy. This will require perseverance in the quest for a truly non-racial South Africa.

However, it begins with you and me making that crucial first step in not polluting children's minds with negative stereotypes and racist attitudes. If we do this we will slowly eradicate racism.

As the 35th President of the United States of America, John F Kennedy said, "All this will not be finished in the first one hundred days. Nor will it be finished in the first one thousand days . . . . nor even perhaps in our lifetime on this planet. But let us begin."[76]

We as a nation must take immediate and sufficient actionable steps to eradicate the scourge of racism.

Finally, I do not say that the views and opinions expressed are 100% correct. I am open to being counselled and educated. However, these are my views and opinions, so let us start a meaningful engagement.

CONCLUSION

A special thank you for reading this book. I hope the book has inspired you to be the catalyst to eradicate racism at all levels of our society. But please do not just pay lip service – take concrete steps to challenge racism at your children's schools, at your church, and at work, and hold your political leaders accountable.

If your organisation is unsure about how to implement anti-racism measures or what the legal requirements are, please contact us at *Siljeur Consulting* (www.siljeurconsulting.co.za), and we will be able to assist.

Racism causes serious hurt. Also, the reputational damage to individuals and institutions can be severe, and they may struggle to recover. It is imperative that all role players in organisations dealing with anti-racism understand the legal requirements and best practices for dealing with breaches of statutory obligations.

Please leave your reviews of this book on Amazon for us to obtain your valuable feedback. Your feedback will assist us in updating this book so that we improve the impact the book can have to eradicate racism.

I hope that you enjoyed reading this book and that, more importantly, you were armed with practical steps you can take to better your environment. If we have done this, please recommend this book to your friends.

ABOUT THE AUTHOR

Nathanael Siljeur is a qualified Advocate of the High Court of South Africa, a qualified accountant, social justice activist, and businessman. He lives with his family in Cape Town.

He has, amongst other qualifications, an MBA and a doctoral degree in law. He is passionate about human rights and social justice issues, and is actively working to create a South Africa where his three children can grow and become powerful testimonies to the potential, creativity, and blessings within them.

His community work includes being the Chairperson of the Board of Management of the Prison Care and Support Network, a non-profit organisation that responds to the spiritual, emotional and educational needs of incarcerated offenders and their families. He is the co-founder and chairperson of the Siljeur Leadership Development Trust, a non-profit organisation focusing on the attainment of socio-economic rights in the Cape Town area. And he is a member of the justice and peace group at his faith sharing community which concentrates on various initiatives involving social justice matters.

Nathanael's company, *Siljeur Consulting*, is available to help organisations with the implementation of anti-racism measures or the completion of independent reviews of organisational procedures and processes. Contact or follow him using the links below:

Company: www.siljeurconsulting.co.za
Personal: www.nathanaelsiljeur.com
LinkedIn: www.linkedin.com/in/nathanael-siljeur-a7478113
Twitter: @sldt4u

ENDNOTES

[1] Citizen reporter. 'Video Racist Adam Catzavelos Finally Breaks Silence', The Citizen, https://citizen.co.za/news/south-africa/1999909/video-racist-adam-catzavelos-finally-breaks-silence (accessed 30 August 2018).

[2] South African Human Rights Commission (SAHRC). 1999. *Fourth Annual Report*. Johannesburg: SAHRC.

[3] Ibid at 3.

[4] South African Human Rights Commission (SAHRC). 1999. *Investigation into Racism in the Media: Interim Report*. Johannesburg: SAHRC.

[5] R Kendall Soulen and Linda Woodhead, (eds). 'Introduction: Contextualising Human Dignity', in *God and Human Dignity*.

[6] Government of Ontario. 'Ontario's 3-year Anti-Racism Plan, a better way forward', at https://www.ontario.ca/page/better-way-forward-ontarios-3-year-anti-racism-strategic-plan (accessed 8 April 2019).

[7] UN General Assembly, International Convention on the Elimination of All Forms of Racial Discrimination, 21 December 1965, United Nations, Treaty Series, vol. 660, p. 195.

[8] Bryan Massingale. 2010. *Racial Injustice and the Catholic Church*. Orbis Books, Maryknoll, New York.

[9] Renni Eddo-Lodge. 2017. Why I'm no longer speaking to white people about race. Bloomsbury, London.

[10] Friederike Bubenzer & Carolin Gomulia. 2018. 'Why the anti-apartheid narrative should include the untold stories of ordinary citizens', News24, accessed 5 May 2019, available at https://www.news24.com/Columnists/GuestColumn/why-the-anti-apartheid-narrative-should-include-the-untold-stories-of-ordinary-citizens-20180424.

[11] Massingale, Racial Injustice and the Catholic Churcha at xiv.

[12] Ruben R Richards. 2018. *Bastaards or human: The unspoken heritage of coloured people,* Volume 1, Origins, identity, culture and challenges.

[13] Lincoln Rice. 2014. Healing the Racial Divide: A Catholic racial injustice framework inspired by Dr Arthur Falls. Pickwick Publications, Eugene, Oregon, at 21.

[14] Brenda Wardle. 2017. Coloured diaries: Experiences of an Eastern Cape 'Mixed Breed' at xvii.

[15] Richards, *Bastaards or human* at 83.

[16] Nicky Falkof. 2016. 'The myth of white purity and narratives that fed racism in South Africa', Wits, available at https://www.wits.ac.za/news/latest-news/in-their-own-words/2016/2016-05/the-myth-of-white-purity-and-narratives-that-fed-racism-in-south-africa.html.

[17] Wardle. 2017, *Coloured diaries* at xxiv.

[18] Richards, *Bastaards or human* at 65.

[19] 'Camissa', Camissa People, https://camissapeople.wordpress.com/camissa (accessed 9 April 2019).

[20] Richards, *Bastaards or human* at 176.

[21] Ibid at 221.

[22] 'Camisa', (https://camissapeople.wordpress.com/camissa) and Richards, *Bastaards or human* at 214.

[23] 'Coloured?', Camissa People, https://camissapeople.wordpress.com/camissa-vs-coloured-challenging-continued-race-labeling (accessed 12 April 2019).

[24] Scott Balson. *The lost tribe of South Africa,* Interactive Presentations (Pty) ltd.

[25] Barbara Pool. 1995. *Die geskiedenis van die Afrikaner-Oorlams in die tyd van Jonker Afrikaner, 1790-1861.* PhD thesis, University of Stellenbosch; Pierre Stoffberg. *Die geskiedenis van die Afrikaner-Oorlams – met spesifieke verwysing na die lewe van Jager (Christiaan) Afrikaner, 1760-1822.* Master's dissertation, University of Stellenbosch.

[26] Ibid.

[27] Ben Magubane. 2001. 'Social Construction of Race and Citizenship in South Africa', a paper prepared for the UNRISD conference on racism and public policy, Durban, South Africa 3-5 September 2001. Available at

http://unrisd.org/80256B3C005BCCF9/(httpAuxPages)/63265CAF F973018D80256B6D005785D1/%24file/dmaguban.pdf (Accessed 9 May 2019).

[28] Sietse Bosgra. 2008. From Jan van Riebeeck to solidarity with the struggle: The Netherlands, South Africa and apartheid.

[29] Helene Opperman Lewis. 2018. *Apartheid: Britains bastard child*, Reach Publishers, at 17.

[30] 'Race classification.' *Apartheid Museum.* Available at https://www.apartheidmuseum.org/race-classification (accessed 12 April 2019).

[31] Francesca Villette, 'The effects of apartheid's unequal education system can still be felt today', IOL, https://www.iol.co.za/capetimes/news/the-effects-of-apartheids-unequal-education-system-can-still-be-felt-today-2035295 (accessed 8 April 2019).

[32] Sampie Terblanche. 2014. Western empires: Christianity, and the inequalities between the West and the rest. Penguin Random House, South Africa.

[33] Dullah Omar, 'Introduction to the Truth and Reconciliation Commission', TRC, available at http://www.justice.gov.za/trc/ (accessed 29 April 2019).

[34] RSA. 1996. *The Constitution of the Republic of South Africa, Act 108, 1996*, Pretoria: Government Printers, available at http://www.acts.co.za/constitution-of/constitution_of_the_republic_o (accessed 8 April 2019).

[35] Ian Currie & Johan De Waal. 2005. *The Bill of Rights handbook.* Fifth edition. Juta.

[36] Allan Boesak. 2015. Public theology lecture, Ujamaa Centre for Biblical and Theological Community Development and Research and the School of Religion, Philosophy and Classics (SRPC), University of KwaZulu-Natal.

[37] Emmy Werner. 2005. 'Resilience and recovery: Findings from the Kauai longitudinal study, research policy, and practice', in *Children's Mental Health,* Summer, Vol. 19, No. 1, 11-14.

[38] Richards. *Bastaards or human* at 43.

[39] Group Areas Act No.41 of 1950.

[40] Nicole Van Driel. 2017. 'The place of Coloured people in the ANC's South Africa', Politicsweb,

http://www.politicsweb.co.za/opinion/the-place-of-coloured-people-in-the-ancs-south-afr (accessed 9 April 2019).

[41] Statistics South Africa. 2017. *Mid-year population estimates* at 2.

[42] Matthews, S., et al. 2004. 'Every six hours a women is killed by her intimate partner: A national study of female homicide in South Africa', *MRC Policy Brief*, No.5 at 2.

[43] Norman Rose. 2009. *Churchill: An unruly life*, Tauris Parke Paperbacks, at 13.

[44] SAHRC.1999. Racism, racial integration and desegregation in South Africa public secondary schools.

[45] Jonathan Jansen. 2018. 'Answer honestly: Would you keep your child in a black-majority school?', available at https://www.dispatchlive.co.za/news/2018-05-10-jonathan-jansen-answer-honestly-would-you-keep-your-child-in-a-black-majority-school/ (accessed 12 April 2019).

[46] Lucien F Longtin & Andrew J Peach. 2017. *Introduction to Catholic ethics.* National Catholic Education Association, at 144.

[47] Karen Pretorius.2019. *Controversial Stellenbosch study on coloured women 'reinforces stereotypes'.* Available at https://www.iol.co.za/weekend-argus/news/controversial-stellenbosch-study-on-coloured-women-reinforces-stereotypes-22620317 (Accessed 9 May 2019).

[48] The Didache Bible with commentaries based on the Catechism of the Catholic Church. Ignatius Bible Edition at 1578.

[49] Bishop Dale J. Melczek. 2003. Created in God's image: Proposal letter on the sin of racism and a call to conversion. Catholic Church, Diocese of Gary at 2.

[50] Harry Flynn. 2003. *In God's image: Pastoral letter on racism.* Diocese of Saint Paul and Minneapolis at 13.

[51] United States Conference of Catholic Bishops. 2018. *Open wide our heart, the enduring call for love*, a pastoral letter against racism.

[52] Pontifical Council for Justice and Peace. *Contribution to World Conference against racism, racial discrimination, xenophobia and related intolerance.* Available at http://www.vatican.va/roman_curia/pontifical_councils/justpeace/documents/rc_pc_justpeace_doc_20010829_comunicato-razzismo_en.html (accessed 8 April 2019).

[53] The McLellan Commission. 2015. *A review of the current safeguarding policies, procedures and practice within the Catholic in Scotland.* Available at

https://www.bcos.org.uk/Portals/0/McLellan/363924_WEB.pdf (accessed 28 July 2018).

[54] The United Church of Canada. 2008. *Ending racial harassment, creating healthy congregation*. Available at https://www.united-church.ca/.../handbook_racial-harassment.pdf (accessed 8 April 2019).

[55] David Isaacson. 'Why Ashwin Willemse is a rare beacon'. *Business Day*. https://www.businesslive.co.za/bd/sport/2018-05-21-why-ashwin-willemse-is-a-rare-beacon/ (accessed 8 April 2019).

[56] Wesley Botton. 'Quota should be a dirty word – sports psychologist'. *The Citizen*. Available at https://citizen.co.za/news/south-africa/1938099/quota-should-be-a-dirty-word-sports-psychologist/ (accessed 8 April 2019).

[57] Sections 15 and 16 of the HRCA.

[58] Section 16 of the HRCA at section 184(2)(a).

[59] Mitra Ebadolahi. 2008. Using structural interdicts and the South African Human Rights Commission to achieve judicial enforcement of economic and social rights in South Africa. New York University School of Law at 1601.

[60] Ibid at 1602.

[61] UN General Assembly. *Universal Declaration of Human Rights*, 10 December 1948, 217 A (III).

[62] Inga T Winkler. *Respect, protect, fulfill: The implementation of the human right to water in South Africa*. Available at http://www.ingawinkler.com/uploads/4/8/6/0/48601803/respect_protect_fulfill.pdf [accessed 13 November 2017] at 423.

[63] Ibid at 424.

[64] SAHRC. *Right to Health – Period: April 2000 – March 2002*, 'Chapter 4 Right to healthcare' at 96. Available at https://www.sahrc.org.za/home/21/files/Reports/4th_esr_chap_4.pdf (accessed 10 April 2019).

[65] Winkler, Respect, protect, fulfill at 425

[66] Government of the Republic of South Africa and Others v Grootboom and Others (CCT11/00) [2000] ZACC 19.

[67] 1998 (1) SA 765 (CC) at para 1.

[68] SA v Grootboom and Others at para 32.

[69] Trispiotis, I. 2010. 'Socio-economic rights: legally enforceable or just aspirational?' *Opticon* 1826 (8) at 4.

[70] Fuo, O. & Du Plessis, A. 2015. 'In the face of judicial deference: Taking the "minimum core" of socio-economic rights to the local government sphere', *L. Dem. & Dev.* vol 19 at 8.

[71] Brand, D. 2011. 'Judicial deference and democracy in socio-economic rights cases in South Africa', *Stell. L. Rev.* vol. 3.

[72] 1998 (1) SA 765 (CC) at para 1.

[73] McLean, K. 2009. Constitutional deference, courts and socio-economic rights in South Africa. Pretoria University Press at 123.

[74] Soobramoney v Minister of Health, KwaZulu-Natal 1998 (1) SA 765 (CC) at para 7.

[75] Government of Ontario, 'Ontario's 3-year Anti-Racism Plan'.

[76] John F. Kennedy. 1961. 'Presidential inaugural address'. Available at https://www.americanrhetoric.com/speeches/jfkinaugural.htm (accessed 19 April 2019).

BIBLIOGRAPHY

Balson, Scott. *The lost tribe of South Africa*, Interactive Presentations (Pty) Ltd.

Boesak, Allan. 2015. Public theology lecture, Ujamaa Centre for Biblical and Theological Community Development and Research and the School of Religion, Philosophy and Classics (SRPC), University of KwaZulu-Natal.

Bosgra, Sietse. 2008. From Jan van Riebeeck to solidarity with the struggle: The Netherlands, South Africa and apartheid.

Botton, Wesley. 'Quota should be a dirty word – sports psychologist'. *The Citizen*. Available at https://citizen.co.za/news/south-africa/1938099/quota-should-be-a-dirty-word-sports-psychologist/ (accessed 8 April 2019).

Brand, D. 2011. 'Judicial deference and democracy in socio-economic rights cases in South Africa', *Stell. L. Rev.* vol. 3.

Bubenzer, F. & Gomulia, Carolin. 2018. 'Why the anti-apartheid narrative should include the untold stories of ordinary citizens', News24, accessed 5 May 2019, available at https://www.news24.com/Columnists/GuestColumn/why-the-anti-apartheid-narrative-should-include-the-untold-stories-of-ordinary-citizens-20180424.

'Camissa', Camissa People, https://camissapeople.wordpress.com/camissa (accessed 9 April 2019).

Citizen reporter. 'Video Racist Adam Catzavelos Finally Breaks Silence', The Citizen, https://citizen.co.za/news/south-africa/1999909/video-racist-adam-catzavelos-finally-breaks-silence (accessed 30 August 2018).

'Coloured?', Camissa People,
https://camissapeople.wordpress.com/camissa-vs-coloured-challenging-continued-race-labeling (accessed 12 April 2019).

Currie, Ian & De Waal, Johan. 2005. *The Bill of Rights handbook*. Fifth edition. Juta.

Ebadolahi, Mitra. 2008. Using structural interdicts and the South African Human Rights Commission to achieve judicial enforcement of economic and social rights in South Africa. New York University School of Law at 1601.

Eddo-Lodge, Renni. 2017. Why I'm no longer speaking to white people about race. Bloomsbury, London.

Falkof, Nicky. 2016. 'The myth of white purity and narratives that fed racism in South Africa', Wits, available at https://www.wits.ac.za/news/latest-news/in-their-own-words/2016/2016-05/the-myth-of-white-purity-and-narratives-that-fed-racism-in-south-africa.html.

Flynn, Harry. 2003. *In God's image: Pastoral letter on racism*. Diocese of Saint Paul and Minneapolis.

Fuo, O. & Du Plessis, A. 2015. 'In the face of judicial deference: Taking the "minimum core" of socio-economic rights to the local government sphere', *L. Dem. & Dev.* vol 19 at 8.

Government of Ontario. 'Ontario's 3-year Anti-Racism Plan, a better way forward', at https://www.ontario.ca/page/better-way-forward-ontarios-3-year-anti-racism-strategic-plan (accessed 8 April 2019).

Government of the Republic of South Africa and Others v Grootboom and Others (CCT11/00) [2000] ZACC 19.

Isaacson, David. 'Why Ashwin Willemse is a rare beacon'. *Business Day*. https://www.businesslive.co.za/bd/sport/2018-05-21-why-ashwin-willemse-is-a-rare-beacon/ (accessed 8 April 2019).

Jansen, Jonathan. 2018. 'Answer honestly: Would you keep your child in a black-majority school?', available at https://www.dispatchlive.co.za/news/2018-05-10-jonathan-jansen-answer-honestly-would-you-keep-your-child-in-a-black-majority-school/ (accessed 12 April 2019).

Kennedy, John F. 1961. 'Presidential inaugural address'. Available at
https://www.americanrhetoric.com/speeches/jfkinaugural.htm
(accessed 19 April 2019).

Longtin, L.F. & Peach, A.J. 2017. *Introduction to Catholic ethics*. National
Catholic Education Association, at 144.

Magubane, Ben. 2001. 'Social Construction of Race and Citizenship
in South Africa', a paper prepared for the UNRISD conference
on racism and public policy, Durban, South Africa 3-5 September
2001. Available at
http://unrisd.org/80256B3C005BCCF9/(httpAuxPages)/63265C
AFF973018D80256B6D005785D1/%24file/dmaguban.pdf
(Accessed 9 May 2019).

Massingale, Bryan. 2010. *Racial Injustice and the Catholic Church*. Orbis
Books, Maryknoll, New York.

Matthews, S., et al. 2004. 'Every six hours a woman is killed by her
intimate partner: A national study of female homicide in South
Africa', *MRC Policy Brief*, No.5 at 2.

McLean, K. 2009. Constitutional deference, courts and socio-
economic rights in South Africa. Pretoria University Press at 123.

Melczek, Bishop Dale J. 2003. Created in God's image: Proposal
letter on the sin of racism and a call to conversion. Catholic
Church, Diocese of Gary.

Omar, Dullah. 'Introduction to the Truth and Reconciliation
Commission', TRC, available at http://www.justice.gov.za/trc/
(accessed 29 April 2019).

Opperman Lewis, Helene. 2018. *Apartheid: Britains bastard child*, Reach
Publishers, at 17.

Pontifical Council for Justice and Peace. *Contribution to World
Conference against racism, racial discrimination, xenophobia and related
intolerance*. Available at
http://www.vatican.va/roman_curia/pontifical_councils/justpea
ce/documents/rc_pc_justpeace_doc_20010829_comunicato-
razzismo_en.html (accessed 8 April 2019).

Pool, Barbara. 1995. *Die geskiedenis van die Afrikaner-Oorlams in die tyd
van Jonker Afrikaner, 1790-1861*. PhD thesis, University of
Stellenbosch.

Pretorius, Karen. 2019. 'Controversial Stellenbosch study on coloured women 'reinforces stereotypes". Available at https://www.iol.co.za/weekend-argus/news/controversial-stellenbosch-study-on-coloured-women-reinforces-stereotypes-22620317 (Accessed 9 May 2019).

'Race classification'. *Apartheid Museum*. Available at https://www.apartheidmuseum.org/race-classification (accessed 12 April 2019).

Report of the world conference against racism, racial discrimination, xenophobia and related intolerance. Available at www.oas.org/dil/afrodescendants_durban_declaration.pdf (accessed 8 April 2019).

Republic of South Africa. 1996. *The Constitution of the Republic of South Africa, Act 108, 1996*, Pretoria: Government Printers, available at http://www.acts.co.za/constitution-of/constitution_of_the_republic_o (accessed 8 April 2019).

Republic of South Africa. Broad-Based Black Economic Empowerment Act 53 of 2003 as amended by Act 46 of 2013.

Republic of South Africa. Employment Equity Act 55 of 1998.

Republic of South Africa. Group Areas Act No.41 of 1950.

Republic of South Africa. Prevention of Unfair Discrimination Act 4 of 2000.

Rice, Lincoln. 2014. Healing the Racial Divide: A Catholic racial injustice framework inspired by Dr Arthur Falls. Pickwick Publications, Eugene, Oregon, at 21.

Richards, Ruben R. 2018. *Bastaards or human: The unspoken heritage of coloured people*, Volume 1, Origins, identity, culture and challenges.

Rose, Norman. 2009. *Churchill: An unruly life*, Tauris Parke Paperbacks, at 13.

SAHRC. *Right to Health – Period: April 2000 – March 2002*, 'Chapter 4 Right to healthcare' at 96. Available at https://www.sahrc.org.za/home/21/files/Reports/4th_esr_chap_4.pdf (accessed 10 April 2019).

SAHRC.1999. Racism, racial integration and desegregation in South Africa public secondary schools.

Soobramoney v Minister of Health, KwaZulu-Natal 1998 (1) SA 765 (CC).

Soulen, R Kendall, and Woodhead, Linda, (eds). 'Introduction: Contextualising Human Dignity', in *God and Human Dignity.*

South African Human Rights Commission (SAHRC). 1999. *Fourth Annual Report.* Johannesburg: SAHRC.

South African Human Rights Commission (SAHRC). 1999. *Investigation into Racism in the Media: Interim Report.* Johannesburg: SAHRC.

Statistics South Africa. 2017. *Mid-year population estimates* at 2.

Stoffberg, Pierre. 1990. *Die geskiedenis van die Afrikaner-Oorlams: Met spesifieke verwysing na die lewe van Jager (Christiaan) Afrikaner, 1760-1822.* MA thesis, University of Stellenbosch.

Terblanche, Sampie. 2014. Western empires: Christianity, and the inequalities between the West and the rest. Penguin Random House, South Africa.

The Didache Bible with commentaries based on the Catechism of the Catholic Church. Ignatius Bible Edition at 1578.

The United Church of Canada. *Ending racial harassment.* https://www.united-church.ca/sites/default/files/resources/handbook_racial-harassment.pdf (accessed 8 April 2019).

The McLellan Commission. 2015. *A review of the current safeguarding policies, procedures and practice within the Catholic in Scotland.* Available at https://www.bcos.org.uk/Portals/0/McLellan/363924_WEB.pdf (accessed 28 July 2018).

The United Church of Canada. 2008. Ending racial harassment, creating healthy congregation. Available at

Trispiotis, I. 2010. 'Socio-economic rights: legally enforceable or just aspirational?' *Opticon* 1826 (8).

UN General Assembly, International Convention on the Elimination of All Forms of Racial Discrimination, 21 December 1965, United Nations, Treaty Series, vol. 660, p. 195.

UN General Assembly. *Universal Declaration of Human Rights*, 10 December 1948, 217 A (III).

United States Conference of Catholic Bishops. 2018. *Open wide our heart, the enduring call for love*, a pastoral letter against racism.

Van Driel, Nicole. 2017. 'The place of Coloured people in the ANC's South Africa', Politicsweb, http://www.politicsweb.co.za/opinion/the-place-of-coloured-people-in-the-ancs-south-afr (accessed 9 April 2019).

Vilette, Francesca. 'The effects of apartheid's unequal education system can still be felt today', IOL, https://www.iol.co.za/capetimes/news/the-effects-of-apartheids-unequal-education-system-can-still-be-felt-today-2035295 (accessed 8 April 2019).

Wardle, Brenda. 2017. Coloured diaries: Experiences of an Eastern Cape 'Mixed Breed' at xvii.

Werner, Emmy. 2005. 'Resilience and recovery: Findings from the Kauai longitudinal study, research policy, and practice', in *Children's Mental Health,* Summer, Vol. 19, No. 1, 11-14.

Winkler, Inga T. *Respect, protect, fulfill: The implementation of the human right to water in South Africa.* Available at http://www.ingawinkler.com/uploads/4/8/6/0/48601803/respect_protect_fulfill.pdf (accessed 13 November 2017).